Happy Are

*Eight Short Studies on
Identity, Destiny and Happiness
in the Beatitudes*

Shan Gastineau

© 2019 by Shan Gastineau shan.gastineau@gmail.com

All rights reserved. No portion of this book may be reproduced, stored in a retrieval system, or transmitted in any form or by any means-electronic, mechanical, photocopy, recording, scanning, or other-except for brief quotations in critical reviews or articles, without the prior written permission of the publisher.

Published in the United States of America

Unless otherwise noted, Scripture quotations are taken from the Holy Bible, New International Version® NIV®. Copyright© 1973, 1978, 1984, 2011 by Biblica, Inc.™ Used by permission of Zondervan. All rights reserved worldwide. www.zondervan.com. The "NIV" and "New International Version" are trademarks registered in the United States Patent and Trademark Office by Biblica, Inc.™

Scriptures marked TM are taken from THE MESSAGE: THE BIBLE IN CONTEMPORARY ENGLISH (TM). Scripture taken from THE MESSAGE: THE BIBLE IN CONTEMPORARY ENGLISH, copyright© 1993, 1994, 1995, 1996, 2000, 2001, 2002. Used by permission of NavPress Publishing Group.

Photography by David Gastineau

Foreword

This work refers often to justice and judicial power, which is fundamental to the promise of realized hope in the Beatitudes - judicial power defined as the legitimate enforcement of the legislated graces through Jesus Christ that have been granted us in both our now God-given identity and God-given destiny. Each chapter stands on its own as an individual study, yet they share a common thread of identity, destiny and conclusively the path to happiness.

In *Our Father*, the first book of this series, a case was made for the judicial power loaded inside the Lord's Prayer. The licit right to enjoy our destiny requires first owning our identity in Jesus. The battle more than anything is a battle for our identity, which at its core is a legal argument in the courtroom of heaven. I can think of few subjects more in the headlines right now than that of identity. So many seem to obsess on available earthly identities that separate and sunder, rather than procuring the one that can liberate and unite. Our heavenly Father seats us in the heavenlies with Christ and has birthed in us a heavenly self. Our adversary presses his bid to drag us down to earth, keeping us strapped and bound to our planet schematics. Our heavenly identity is truth. Our earthly identity, though factual, has now become false, if it contradicts and conflicts with the new creation. Not that it isn't important, quite the contrary. Because we are such flesh and blood, getting release from earthly identities is not humanly possible, but requires supernatural intervention. We, however, have a significant role to play, vigilantly affirming our gifted truth and facing down the liar with our Lawyer. This second volume continues the theme of identity and destiny, **with the promise of a state of being that all of humanity has been striving for since creation.**

Blessed Are

The first two words in all of the eight Beatitudes are "Blessed are" or "Happy are." The title is meant to be a poor play on the phrase Happy Hour. There also is a purpose in the choice of photographs for the cover of this book, though I can't help but admit that provoking religious spirits was a secondary benefit. Antagonizing modern Pharisees is irresistible.

Blessedness, or more accurately happiness, is the object of the celebrated eight Beatitudes presented by Jesus. Could any other picture more accurately portray the antithesis of Jesus' teaching in the Beatitudes? A mobster represents the opposite of every path to happiness as submitted here. Poverty, mourning, meekness, hungering and thirsting for righteousness, mercy, purity in heart, peace-making, rejoicing when persecuted are almost laughable in how much they intuit counter to human convention. To even remotely be persuaded that Jesus is on to something here requires a complete re-wiring of the human brain and reinvention so sweeping that the old neural paths are paved over with new highways. His postulates in the Beatitudes require backhoes for the heart, earthmovers in the mind and bulldozers for the brain.

The Sermon on the Mount, considered by many to be the most beautiful of speeches, was given sometime early in Jesus's itinerant ministry. The speech began with these Beatitudes on the side of a mountain overlooking the Sea of Galilee and he offered what has gone down in history as either the most sublime words ever spoken, or due to its impossibility of attainment, a great stand-up routine. It does not fall anywhere in between. If it were comedy, the Beatitudes would be Johnny Carson's opening monologue, with Ed McMahon laughing uproariously in the background.

But it was not comedy, certainly not to the many who were early on paraded out as lunch for lions, or lit up like torches by Nero, or more preferably beheaded. They took these words to be absolute truth. Happiness was their object.

The worn human paths to happiness have been discredited for millennia, yet every generation continues to rub these same routes down so deeply that the shoulders of the road now rise above our heads. The grooves in our grey matter have been genetically passed on to us and breaking the cycle requires non-human intervention. Add to this something psychologists call the **hedonic treadmill.** Also known as **hedonic adaptation,** the hedonic treadmill is the observed tendency of humans to quickly return to a relatively stable level of happiness despite major positive or negative events or life changes. According to this theory, as a person makes more money, expectations and desires rise in tandem, which results in no permanent gain in happiness.[1]

The concept dates back centuries, to such writers as St. Augustine, and given that hedonic adaptation generally demonstrates that a person's long-term happiness is not significantly affected by otherwise impacting events, positive psychology has concerned itself with the discovery of things that can lead to lasting changes in happiness levels.

On-line search the word happiness and you may now see headlines on how over-rated seeking happiness is. You may also see psychologists pushing other foci that hold hope of satisfaction, so elusive is the sustaining of the thoroughly enjoyable chemical reaction in our person when experiencing happiness. No wonder it seems to make sense to change the end rather than the means. If you keep missing the target, then move the darn target. We humans are clearly resistant to exploring other means to the happiness end, so let's redefine the end. I predict that dumbing down the objective will prove as fruitless.

Why do we continue with such self-defeating behaviors and not consider a radical approach to redefining the paths to happiness?

Even in business, if you listed the biggest challenges you face, surely on that list would be the pace of change, the short life span of a technological edge, the rapid commoditization of the products and services your company brings to market, and the diminishing effectiveness of past strategies. As trite as it sounds, change seems to be the only constant, or more specifically the regular reinvention required to stay relevant.

If I don't subject my business to rigorous examination and regularly reinvent myself, someone else most certainly will put me out of business. I have personally had to reinvent myself four different times throughout my business career. It can also be done in the human heart. Getting stuck in our ways is an age-old dilemma, and neatly validated by what happens in the dorsal striatum region of our brains. But it is no longer an acceptable excuse for an inability to adapt and change to what actually works.

Maybe Jesus was on to something. Just maybe the ways to happiness proposed by Christ were always the ways, but humans early on took detours that have now turned into boulevards with supporting infrastructure, development and government incentives. Now, the way of the Beatitudes is the detour. Regardless, our way is not working, but just giving a new way a try will not suffice. Reinvention requires commitment. As the old saw goes about preparing a breakfast of ham and eggs, "the chicken was involved, but the pig was committed." This book is meant to make just that case, the case for our commitment. Nothing short of that will generate the re-paving of the paths to happiness and the reinvention of who we are and what we do to obtain the thing we are all after.

Introduction

A first principle is a basic, foundational, self-evident proposition or assumption that cannot be deduced from any other proposition or assumption. In philosophy, first principles are taught by Aristotelians, and nuanced versions of first principles are referred to as postulates by Kantians.

Is happiness truly a first principle as posited by the ancient philosophers? That all humans wish for happiness is a fundamental assumption of Socratic, as well as Platonic and Aristotelian, moral psychology. In Plato's *Symposium*, the lover loves and desires good and beautiful things to possess them for himself, and this because he wishes to be happy; for happiness consists in the possession of good things. So if one asks the lover why he loves beautiful things, the answer is that he wishes to be happy, and this answer is final, in that one cannot ask for what purpose someone wishes to be happy and expect a further answer.[2]

Even in the case for American autonomy, one of our eloquent founders stated first principles in our Declaration of Independence –

"We hold these truths to be self-evident, that all men are created equal, that they are endowed by their Creator with certain unalienable Rights, that among these are Life, Liberty and the pursuit of Happiness."

The English word *happiness* suggests a feeling-state that differs from pleasure only in being more serene and prolonged, but its etymological connection *hap* (archaic word for luck or fortune), *happen*, and *hapless* preserves the memory of an earlier force. *Happiness* also has an objective sense: well-being, the state of affairs in which things are well with a person, however they feel. Though, the state of having "good hap" has an irreducible connotation of fortune or luck in the English word that is not present in the Greek.[3]

Beatitudes, which comes from the Latin *beatitudines*, translates happy, rich and blessed; and are so called because Jesus begins each of the eight promises with the word *blessed*. The original Greek word, *makarios*, does indeed translate well as happy, rich and blessed, with emphasis upon happy. The more common New Testament Greek word for blessed is *eulogetos*, which is a powerful word in its own right. However, the use by Matthew of *makarios*, which is a translation of the Aramaic *tuba* used by Jesus, fits beautifully. *Tuba* in descending order of definitions begins with 1) glory, then 2) fruits and income, 3) wealth and resources, 4) happiness and blessedness. With all the wonderful choices to make in translating from Aramaic to Greek, and Greek to English, *blessed* was obviously chosen and the rest is history. Some renegade translators do more appropriately translate the Greek to English as *happy*, but that doesn't feel as eloquent or religious. Oh, how I love religious spirits. You have seen the title of this book and where I land with the translators should be clear. This is a book on the first principle of happiness. Jesus implies that happiness is irreducible and the end object of our desire. In his inimitable way, he dramatically demarks how to obtain this elusive state.

Operating from a heavenly platform is the next great evolution of the church. It has always been there, but the power of our flesh and blood to keep us earth bound is not to be trifled with. The old criticism of Christians that they were so heavenly minded they were no earthly good does not apply here. The objective is to be heavenly present and earthly empowered, maximizing the opportunity for good upon the earth with all the importunity of heaven.

"Forget the former things; do not dwell on the past. See I am doing a new thing! Now it springs up, do you not perceive it? I am making a way in the desert and streams in the wasteland." (Isaiah 43:18,19)

Jesus came to reveal a new way. The Hebrew standard of God's power had ever been the crossing of the Red Sea upon departing Egypt. God says now to forget the old way. Rather than turn the sea into a desert, he is going to turn the desert into a sea. The old way was trying to impact heaven from earth and now it will be impacting earth from heaven. Get ready!

Hedonia vs. Eudaimonia

What a culture considers significant is often nuanced with synonyms yielding shades of subtleties. Not unlike the indigenous peoples of the Arctic, which have some 50 different words for snow, the Greeks had many words for happiness. As might be surmised, with the different ancient terms for happiness, the Greeks were obsessed with obtaining it.

Though neither of these two ancient Greek words and concepts are explicitly used in the Beatitudes, they are descriptive relative to this discussion. Both are prescribed by time, meaning one term is defined in the moment and the other defined at the end. *Hedonia*, as you might expect, since its obvious cognate is hedonism, is pleasure or happiness obtained in the moment or near future. *Eudaimonia* on the other hand cannot be measured until the end of someone's life. One cannot have lived a life of happiness only to end in great misfortune and be described as having had a life of *eudaimonia*.

Research on well-being can be thought of as falling into two traditions. In one – the hedonistic tradition – the focus is on happiness, generally defined as the presence of positive affect and the absence of negative affect. In the other – the eudaimonic tradition – the focus is on living life in a full and deeply satisfying way.

The primary difference between *hedonia* and *eudaimonia* can be described as "feel-good" vs. "feel-purpose." I have not heard any definition that better sums up the two. In the context of building a culture of contentment inside a business, hedonic and eudaimonic pathways both play a crucial role in order to keep employees fully engaged and productive – but most measures that foster hedonic experiences are rather short-lived, and perhaps even more important, easy to copy by competitors – whereas conditions that foster meaning and purpose are rather hard to replicate.[4]

Hedonia in short, is about pleasure, enjoyment, satisfaction and the absence of distress. *Eudaimonia* is about authenticity, meaning, excellence and personal growth.

So where does *makarios*, the word used by the Gospel writer, fit into this discussion. Aristotle takes a crack at it in his great work *Nicomachean Ethics*. He explores at length a definition of *eudaimonia* and then wonders where *makarios* fits into his theories on happiness. He hints that the differences are few, but that *eudaimonia* seems to be happiness for humans on earth and *makarios* is happiness for the gods. The word used for happiness in the Beatitudes would be completely appropriate if considered a divine blessedness experienced by earthly humans. This is certainly one of the better arguments for choosing "blessed are" rather than "happy are." Blessed has such a divine note to it.

Self-Interest

Many, maybe all, philosophic, economic, and political systems are built upon a supposition of human disposition. Are humans innately good or innately evil? Pre-supposing that humans are innately good and devising systems that require that predicate have repeatedly disappointed. The pre-supposition that humans are innately bad may come closer to observed history but devising human schemes around that also produces largely failed shame cultures. What seems clear is that human nature is irredeemably self-interested. Any attempt to mock-up an economic, political, or spiritual system that does not include the predicate of human self-interest will fail. C.S. Lewis said,

"If we consider the unblushing promises of reward and the staggering nature of the rewards promised in the Gospels, it would seem that Our Lord finds our desires not too strong, but too weak. We are half-hearted creatures fooling about with drink and sex and ambition when infinite joy is offered us, like an ignorant child who wants to go on making mud pies in a slum because he cannot image what is meant by the offer of a holiday at the sea."[5]

Jesus's divine brilliance did not attempt to surgically remove human self-interest, but unabashedly promoted a belief system that masterfully wove such interest into its very core. Rewards abound. Unfortunately, many of his disciples today preach a gospel of selflessness that misses the mark of self-wellness and the beautiful and sacrificial acts that can proceed out of the same. Jesus didn't even attempt to re-define the result. Happiness is happiness. It needs no definition, or any re-defining. Repeatedly through-out his three-year ministry, Jesus taught a new approach, authoritatively proclaiming a new path of self-interest. The end is the same. The means have changed. He began with the Beatitudes.

I

Blessed are the poor in spirit: for theirs is the kingdom of heaven

Or, *the kingdom of heaven is theirs.* The old saw that Christians were so heavenly minded they were no earthly good, back in the day had some basis in fact. The evolution of the church taking place today is that **Christians are learning to be heavenly present so they can be earthly empowered.** All the power and authority available to a citizen of the kingdom is in their possession. What is a kingdom if not the dominion of a king? Remember that classical Greek philosophers defined happiness as the possession of good things. Jesus has offered up what one of those good things are, the custody of the kingdom of heaven. Sounds like a good thing to me but what does it mean?

Time or Place?

This will be the first of a few beatitudes that have been historically interpreted relative to time more than to place. Nothing about time is mentioned here but is it not assumed that Jesus must be talking about the future since he is talking about heaven? That could be our first mistake. Maybe Jesus is talking about eternity, but he is also speaking of the present. And without contradiction he is talking about a location and a place. Heaven is bustling with activity right now. Angels are in joyful assembly, the church of the inheritance is present with their names written in heaven, God the judge of all is presiding, the spirits of the just made perfect are in attendance, the mediator of the New Covenant is ready with his sprinkled blood that speaks better things than that of Abel (Hebrews 12:22-24). The author of Hebrews doesn't tell us to come on up, on the contrary, he (she?) asserts that we have already arrived.

Moreover, the author continues that since we are presently taking possession of an unshakable kingdom, let us give thanks and offer pleasing service to God (Hebrews 12:28).

Don't know about you but for most of my walk with Jesus, which was often in defeat and retreat, I wasn't cavorting with angels, or frequenting with the church of the firstborn, or hanging out with the spirits of the just ones made perfect, least of all daily consulting with my mediator regarding what his blood is speaking and what that means for others and me. And on that subject - just what is the sprinkled blood of Jesus saying and to whom is the blood speaking?

A Better Vengeance

The book of Hebrews makes the case for better throughout and uses the word 13 times. Better than angels; better than Moses; a better high priest; a better covenant; a better sacrifice; a better salvation; better promises and better things. We have come to the blood of sprinkling that speaks **better things** than that of Abel (Hebrews 12:24).

Let's consider first what the blood of Abel had to say. Most know the story of Cain and Abel, the sons of Adam and Eve. After the fall Cain and Abel offered different sacrifices to God – Cain's sacrifice was rejected and Abel's was received. Why the difference is not the object here, but what happens next is - Cain in his anger and spite murders his brother (Genesis 4:1-8).

"Then the Lord said to Cain, 'Where is your brother Abel?' 'I don't know,' he replied. 'Am I my brother's keeper?' The Lord said, 'What have you done? Listen! Your brother's blood cries out to me from the ground.'" (Genesis 4:9,10)

Abel's blood was speaking vengeance and retribution, seeking justice. Continuing with Cain, the Lord said,

"Now you are under a curse and driven from the ground, which opened its mouth to receive your brother's blood from your hand. When you work the ground, it will no longer yield its crops for you. You will be a restless wanderer on the earth." (Genesis 4:11,12)

The author of Hebrews states we have a better high priest- better and different - but still a high priest. We have better covenant and better promises, but still a covenant and promises. The sprinkled blood speaks better things than that of Abel - the Book of Hebrews is a comparison between the better and heavenly vs the inferior and earthly. The blood of Jesus doesn't speak the opposite of Abel, it speaks the same thing, only better and heavenly. The blood of Abel spoke earthly vengeance and the blood of Jesus speaks heavenly vengeance. Have we ever considered that the blood of Jesus is speaking vengeance on our behalf? Blood demands justice.

The kingdom of heaven that we have taken possession of is more than anything a kingdom of justice, a kingdom that makes things right. A kingdom that rescues that which has been captured, returns that which has been taken, retrieves that which has been plundered, recovers that which has been lost, repairs that which has been broken and rebuilds that which has been torn down.

Hear the Messianic Isaiah 35 –

"Be strong, do not fear; your God will come with vengeance; with divine retribution he will come to save you." (Isaiah 35:3)

To the ancient Hebrews, salvation for God's people was synonymous to punishment for the enemies of God's people. They were always one and the same. You could not have one without the other. This messianic prophecy says Christ will appear with vengeance and divine retribution. What? Then the prophet lays out in detail what this vengeance looks like,

The eyes of the blind will be opened, the ears of the deaf unstopped, the lame will leap like a deer, the mute tongue will shout for joy, water will gush forth in your wilderness and streams in your desert, the burning sand will become a pool, the thirsty ground will become bubbling springs. (Isaiah 35:5-7)

The Seer saw into the future and painted a picture of the Messianic mission of vengeance. His mission on earth would above all be retribution against the spiritual enemy that had bound up the human soul with sin and human flesh with infirmity. The blood of Abel cried out for earthly vengeance against an earthly enemy. The blood of Jesus demands heavenly vengeance against a spiritual enemy.

"Do not take revenge, my friends, but leave room for God's wrath, for it is written: 'It is mine to avenge; I will repay,' says the Lord." (Romans 12:19)

To possess the kingdom of heaven is to access the power and authority of God's kingdom, which is to employ the blood of Christ, which speaks justice and retribution on our behalf, in the Judge's presence, against spiritual rulers, against authorities, against the powers of this dark world and against the spiritual forces of evil in the heavenly realms. (Ephesians 6:12)

The first promise of happiness is the availability of the power and authority of the kingdom of heaven. If you prefer to wait until the next life, that is fine. Those who would also like to see what that means this side of eternity will do better.

Wisdom

In 469 BC, Socrates was born and, though leaving nothing written down (as far as we know), came to be regarded along with his student Plato as the fathers of western philosophy. His student Plato's influence was so vast that,

"The safest general characterization of the European philosophical tradition is that it consists of a series of footnotes to Plato."[6]

70 years later, in 399 BC, Socrates perished inside an Athenian prison with many of his closest friends, students and admirers at his side. The trial before a rigged jury of 500 and the subsequent unjust conviction was sufficient even for his city to quietly permit him to escape prison and spend the rest of his life in exile. He declined, reasoning that it would be unjust to have spent his life enjoying the benefits of his great city to then not be subject to its laws when they punished him.

The great philosopher, who went about bare-foot and in ragged clothing, impoverished by choice, challenged his fellow citizens, who were consumed with making money and making war, to pursue the things of the soul rather than the things of the body - to pursue and comprehend virtues like justice, courage, temperance, prudence, love and friendship. To embrace the immortality of the soul.

Socrates put his fellow citizens generally into two buckets. The common denominator with both was that they didn't know anything. Not things like making money and making war, but that they didn't know anything about the virtues of the soul. The first bucket was full of people who didn't know that they didn't know anything. This bucket held the sweeping majority. Bucket number two contained people who knew that they didn't know anything. Socrates considered himself wiser than most simply because he put himself in that bucket, he knew that he didn't know anything. This was the point of beginning for any and all who would seek wisdom and to apprehend the great virtues of the immortal soul.

The point of beginning for wisdom was an emptiness of mind and soul, an abject poverty of intellect and spirit, that would give birth to the inquiry required to make progress. This is the first proposed path to happiness. Unfortunately, human disposition what it is, failure is often prescribed to birth such poverty - thus the saying that wisdom is the daughter of failure and the mother of success. I am not sure that failure really teaches, but it surely unteaches.

"It's not what we don't know that gets us into trouble. It's what we know for sure that just ain't so." (Mark Twain)

Moros, Mora, Moron

The Greek adjective for foolish in every linguistic gender ... in 1955 a *moros* boy was born. This was not his heavenly and God-given identity, but very much a part of his earthly genetic code. Though he started life with many self-doubts and insecurities, by the time he rolled into his late teen-age years he was increasing in absolute self-certainty. Even becoming a Christian at 17 years old did not de-rail the sense of self-rightness, possibly only increasing the certainty of every held opinion. This young man was certain about almost everything, certain enough to think he could pastor a church when all of 19 years old, self-assured as a spiritual leader, husband and a father. Becoming autodidactic at everything, submitting to a mentor was out of the question. Getting divorced at 27 and leaving the ministry shortly thereafter temporarily shook his confidence, but he quickly subsumed those doubts with falsely inflamed courage and bravado, facing the new world with a simmering rage that was hidden manipulatively beneath a socially functional façade.

20 years later, as the failures of character mounted, the anger burned out, and at 47 years old he declared spiritual and intellectual bankruptcy. Not the Chapter 11 reorganization variety. But Chapter 7 bankruptcy, the complete liquidation of every held belief, opinion, and certainty. Jesus had promised the abundant life, but there was nothing resembling abundance for this man at any level ... spirit, soul or body. His self-driven, self-taught, self-certain approach to all had belatedly brought him to this thorough and fully impoverished state. He chose to hold onto Jesus Christ and him crucified. Every other held belief was up for grabs, so complete was his defeat.

Finally, he was poor in spirit, poor in soul, and poor in mind. He knew that he didn't know anything. What could have and should have happened at 17 when he began with Christ, didn't happen until he was 47. Like so much tattered clothing, the old self the Apostle Paul speaks of in Ephesians had never been removed. The new self had never had an opportunity to form in Christ. Spending the next two years in grief, tears and repentance had nothing to do with not being forgiven by the Lord, but very much to do with the stripping away of the false and phony man, the old man of this present age that thought he knew everything, not even remotely perceiving that he knew nothing.

This is my story - the spiritual and intellectual bankruptcy which became the place of beginning for Christ to form in me. I was finally poor in spirit.

Receive or Take

There is a beautiful vignette tucked into the rear third of John chapter three. After Jesus reveals to Nicodemus truth about God's love and spiritual birth, the evangelist shifts to the later stage of John the Baptist's ministry, before King Herod throws him in prison and cuts off his head. Jesus ministry has commenced and some of John's disciples observe to the Baptist that his ministry is in decline and everyone is going to the new guy. To that John says –

"A man can receive only what is given him from heaven." (John 3:27)

And then,

"He must become greater; I must become less." (John 3:30)

Verse 27 brings up so many questions. What does given from heaven mean? Can we know in advance what it is that we have been given? When do we receive it? How do we receive it? And left out here many other questions about this over-the-top provocative comment from John.

Once again, we have a conundrum with the rich and varied vocabulary of the English language. Half of our language comes from Old French and the other half comes from Old English, which is derived from both Old Germanic and Old Norse words. "Receive" in the Greek language, *lambano*, means both to take and to receive. There is little distinction in the New Testament between the two English words. They only differ for English speakers because we have two words to choose from, *receive*, which comes from Old French, and *take*, which comes from Old Norse. The many years of having both words to choose from has given a more active and aggressive definition to the word *take* and a more passive tone to the word *receive*. *Receive* seems to require a giver, where to *take* doesn't require that someone give. To the Greeks, *lambano* meant to take something and possess it, or attempt to possess it regardless of whether the other party was freely giving it. Receiving something in the New Testament is a very aggressive, active taking of something and possessing it for oneself. That is an important distinction to our watered-down English word descended from Old French that feels less violent.

Furthermore, can we know from our heavenly Father in advance what it is that has been granted to us so we may then with confidence, and regardless of the obstacles, or with all signs to the contrary, go take it and possess it? This was certainly the case with John the Baptist who offered this nugget. Plainly he knew his destiny and God's plan for him in advance. He may not have known every daily detail, but he held the big picture rock solid. He then went out, took it, received it, possessed it and lived it out, possibly even knowing how it would end.

The other option is to not know in advance from our Father in heaven what it is that we have been given, which then produces these possible outcomes.

1) We go through life asking that God's will for us be done and let life's experiences and outcomes interpret for us what that looks like. Open door … it must be God. Closed door … not his will. This seems to be the modus operandi of most committed Christians.

2) Because we don't know from God what it is that we have been given, we probably spend valuable time and energy trying to receive and take that which has not been granted to us.
3) Worse yet, because we don't know from God what is that we have been given, we don't spend valuable time and energy receiving and taking that which has been granted to us.

However, we could take Paul the Apostle up on his admonition to not be foolish but to understand what the will of the Lord is. Consistent with the thesis of the first book in this series, the better option is to go to heaven, present ourselves to the Father, seek a download of our destiny, and with the authority of the kingdom of heaven and empowered by the Holy Spirit, go take hold of and possess it, brightly living out our irrevocable calling. Of all the things I was so certain about in life, this is the one area where I was short of sureness. It would have been so much better to be sure of my destination and unsure of all those other things. That would have been wisdom indeed.

For Discussion

1. Take a moment to discuss the kingdom of heaven, things that stand out to you in this chapter, questions you have questions about and things you feel directed to do.
2. Discuss the concept of a "better" vengeance.
3. What does poor in spirit mean to you? What are some certainties that you have held that need reevaluation?
4. The concepts of giving and taking are combined in one New Testament Greek word. What are the similarities and differences of the two in English?
5. Do you think it is possible to know from God in advance what it is that you have been given from heaven? If so, what could that look like in your life?

II

Blessed are they that mourn: for they shall be comforted

The Paraklete

No, not the parakeet, but the *Paraklete* (Greek *parakletes*) ... the term used especially by the Apostle John to describe Jesus and the Holy Spirit. This neat Greek word has so many nuances of meaning - advocate, comforter, encourager, but is consistently translated advocate for Jesus in John's first epistle and comforter for the Holy Spirit in John's gospel. To John, both Jesus and the Holy Spirit argue on our behalf. Yes, they comfort and encourage, but they emphatically advocate on our behalf. That is how we are most comforted and encouraged, when there is an argument for us demanding enforcement of our legitimate son-ship and daughter-ship. Our Lord and the Holy Spirit are our Lawyers-in-Chief. Paul says,

"In the same way, the Spirit helps us in our weakness. We do not know what we ought to pray for, but the Spirit himself intercedes for us with groans that words cannot express." (Romans 8:26)

Parakaleo is the beautiful cognate verb of the noun *paracletes*. Literally parsed, *parakaleo* translates to call to one's side, and *paracletes*, one who is called to one's side. More specifically – *Lidell and Scott Greek-English Lexicon* defines the word accordingly, *to summon one's friends to attend one in a trial, to be summoned to attend at a trial.* It later softens into *call to, exhort, cheer, encourage, comfort, console.* The Apostle John favors the primary legal meaning, both in his gospel and his first letter.

When I think of the modern, watered down, lukewarm, milquetoast definition of the word "comfort," it leans more towards sympathy, which is fine when sympathy is called for. Could Jesus really be saying here that those who mourn will be happy because they will receive sympathy? I hope not! Maybe comfort means to make comfortable. Blessed are those who mourn for they shall be made comfortable. Hmmm. If I have suffered at the hands of injustice, or have fallen prey to unfortunate circumstances, or have lost loved ones, sympathy and comfortability are very appealing. However, I don't see that as happiness. If as the ancient philosophers believed, that happiness is the obtaining of good things, then I would think the good thing in this regard is something far larger than feeling better after feeling bad.

Oaks of Justice

Attending his hometown synagogue, Jesus began to read about himself out loud from what is now Isaiah chapter 61. He didn't read the entire passage ... he didn't need to. Every listening Jew knew by the heart the famous promises in this passage. Messiah would come and be the final and perfect fulfillment of the Year of Jubilee, which year we described in the book *Our Father*. Here are the well memorized verses that needed little explanation, except that the town of Nazareth had a hard time accepting their home-town boy was the one.

"The Spirit of the Sovereign Lord is on me, because the Lord has anointed me to preach good news to the poor. He has sent me to bind up the brokenhearted, to proclaim freedom for the captives and release from darkness for the prisoners, to proclaim the year of the Lord's favor (Year of Jubilee) and the day of vengeance of our God, **to comfort all who mourn, and provide for those who grieve in Zion** – to bestow on them a crown of beauty instead of ashes, the oil of gladness instead of mourning, and a garment of praise instead of a spirit of despair. They will be called oaks of righteousness (justice), a planting of the Lord for the display of his splendor." (Isaiah 61:1-3, parentheses and bold mine)

I admit to these being my favorite verses in the entire Bible. In this passage the entire ministry of Jesus is summed. Evidently, a large part of that ministry was to comfort those who mourn and to provide for those who grieve.

And,

Legal restoration to one's destiny; a royal crown of beauty to redeem the torched life; the anointing oil of gladness to follow the mourning; a judicial garment of praise to replace the despair; and lastly, the mourners will be called Oaks of Justice.

When Jesus in the Sermon on the Mount used the phrase *for they shall be comforted*, these verses from Isaiah are what the audience heard. – They heard legal restoration, they heard vengeance, they heard a royal crown, they heard an anointing oil of authority, they heard a judicial robe, and they heard oaks of justice.

Try on for size this translation of the second beatitude –

Happy are those who mourn for they shall be advocated for.

I warned you in my first book once you put Kingdom glasses on you see the legal authority and judicial power in almost every breath of the Bible.

The description in the gospels of the ministry of Jesus is exemplified by comfort, though there are no indications that he ever put his arm around someone to console them. It was prophesied that he would provide for those who mourn, but there are no stories of him showing up at a wake with food. He was sent to comfort those who grieve, but he didn't send cards or flowers to the sick or dying. He didn't offer grief counseling. There is only one record of him offering a eulogy and that was for his cousin, John the Baptist. Jesus defined comfort in a way that no one before him had. Comfort was advocacy and his advocacy produced joy. How he went about advocating and comforting was beautifully expressed when his cousin sent two of his disciples to Jesus to ask if he was the expected one?

"Go back and report to John what you have seen and heard: The blind receive sight, the lame walk, those who have leprosy are cured, the deaf hear, the dead are raised, and the good news is preached to the poor." (Luke 7:22)

Those who mourn need heavenly advocacy, one who can stand before God on their behalf and make a case for justice. That is what being comforted really is.

"He will not judge by what he sees with his eyes or decide by what he hears with his ears, but with righteousness he will judge the needy, with justice he will give decisions for the poor of the earth." (Isaiah 11:3,4)

To Label is To Enable?

Or so I thought for much of my life. My old dysfunctional self thought that by acknowledging difficult feelings, hurts or fears was to empower them. That also put me in the precarious position of refusing to acknowledge the difficult feelings, hurts and fears of others. To acknowledge them was to label them and to label them was to enable them in my life or their lives. Was I the only one like this? To compound the problem, though it seemed rational at the time, the feelings often were not coming from a place of truth, therefore the feelings did not deserve acknowledgement of reality. How messed up can someone be? Surely this thinking proceeded out of my twisted notion of courage that had been built on a lie. To be courageous was to ignore the feelings and emotions as false because they proceeded from a false place. No wonder my emotional quotient was so low.

Blessed are they that mourn? Mourning and grief are plainly a place of feeling that we would prefer to avoid. Or if unavoidable, then finding an exit ramp out of the feeling as quickly as possible. Maybe Jesus was on to something. For sure, the ancients knew how to mourn and express grief. Or so it would seem when you read them. There were tragedies and comedies, either crying or laughing, and at the extremes. It was possible upon the death of a loved one to hire professional mourners who knew how to wail. Grief was big business, even then.

I guess I have come full circle; from emotionally closed-up and bound-up, unable to acknowledge negative feelings nor wanting to empower them - to at least grasping there had to be a better way.

Now it is time to give that awfulness a name. Sad? Anxious? Angry? I do hesitate to refer too much to neuroscience for two reasons; it is not my field of expertise and the study of the brain in this regard is in its infancy. Anything written about it could become quickly dated. I prefer to stick to concepts that can stand the test of time. Regardless, here goes.

In a study, participants viewed pictures of people with emotional facial expressions. Predictably, each participant's amygdala activated to the emotions in the picture. But when they were asked to name the emotion, the ventrolateral prefrontal cortex activated and reduced the emotional amygdala reactivity. In other words, consciously recognizing the emotions reduced their impact.[7]

Suppressing emotions doesn't work and can backfire on you.

A study found that people who tried to suppress a negative emotional experience failed to do so. While they thought they looked fine outwardly, inwardly their limbic system was just as aroused as without suppression, and in some cases, even more aroused. Trying not to feel something doesn't work, and in some cases even backfires.[8]

But labeling, on the other hand, makes a big difference.

To reduce arousal, you need to use just a few words to describe an emotion, and ideally use symbolic language using indirect metaphors, metrics and simplifications of your experience. This requires you to activate your prefrontal cortex, which reduces the arousal in the limbic system. Here is the bottom line: describe an emotion in just a word or two, and it helps reduce the emotion.[9]

Hoary methods have been way ahead of us. Meditation has employed this for centuries. Labeling is a fundamental tool of mindfulness. In fact, labeling affects the brain so powerfully it works with other people too. Labeling emotions is one of the primary tools use by FBI hostage negotiators.

A Time to Mourn?

"A time to weep and a time to laugh, a time to mourn and a time to dance." (Ecclesiastes 3:4)

There is a time to mourn and a time for grief. If not your grief, then someone else's. In this beatitude,

Jesus appears to link lament with heavenly advocacy. Maybe it is mourning that activates advocacy like few other environments.

"Rejoice with those who rejoice, mourn with those who mourn." (Romans 12:16)

But it is more than just the Latin compassion or the Greek sympathy, which both mean to feel together with someone. We symbiotically enter into what someone feels so we may serve as a *parakletes* along with the Holy Spirit to intercede on their behalf and see God speak into their life. It is human nature to want an egress from grief as quickly as possible, thinking grief to be more destructive than it is healing. Indeed, one can get trapped in a seeming interminable cycle of grief that we could all agree is not healthy. However, attempting to exit grief as quickly as possible may be just as unhealthy. There is something deeply restorative, indeed even purifying, when in a sustained season of grief and mourning, though we are so possibly afraid of pernicious depression that we may leave too early.

James, the brother of Jesus, advises that not only do we not too quickly leave grief, but there are seasons we should proactively enter into mourning. It might be hyperbole to say that I have never observed this in any believer community - to activate grief, to reject for a season joy and laughter, and uncover what the power of mourning and tears can do.

"Grieve, mourn and wail. Change your laughter to mourning and your joy to gloom. Humble yourselves before the Lord, and he will lift you up." (James 4:9,10)

I am Crucified

Becoming a Christian in 1973, I soon made a dash for the wilderness. Though faith meant much to me, I wandered selfishly and aimlessly for the next 30 years. Then decisively coming to the place of utter spiritual and intellectual poverty, I was at last ready to give everything to Jesus and receive everything he had for me. I spent the next two years in grief and repentance. Knowing I was forgiven my wandering was not the point. Intuitively sensing that a season of grief and mourning were required, I camped out there purposely, rejecting any attempt to exit prematurely. Two years later, with my wife terribly tired of it all, I felt a release to come out. With Jewish friends we attended Yom Kippur at synagogue that fall and I walked out a free man. The two years of grief had much to do with getting the old fake man on the cross. Though it is for sure an on-going and daily experience, that first real crucifixion took some leaning into. First the feet, then one hand, then the next. Then the suffocation process of crucifixion, which is what the death process really is. Inhaling is easy, it is the exhaling that is so hard. In agony and pain, trying to lift yourself up while hanging on the cross so your lungs can exhale air. Then you inhale. Then lift yourself up again to exhale, then inhale. Finally, the lifting up that allows the lungs to exhale becomes too difficult, then impossible. At last, suffocation and death. When Paul says in Galatians 2:20 that "I am crucified with Christ" he had done and was continuing to spiritually do something that took time and was painful. After 30 years of wandering in the wilderness I was ready – so tired of not having the abundant life, which was impossible to have, as long as the old man was still breathing. I had no abundant life because I had never experienced abundant death. On earth death comes after life. In Christ's kingdom life comes after death. I now carry that two years of grief and mourning with me as a powerful memory, even a prized memory in my walk with Jesus. I came out of that process transformed and on fire. The power of inhaling is only as strong as the power to exhale. Any person with asthma can tell you that. It ain't about the inhale, it's about the exhale. Inhaling is easy once the lungs are empty. I had spent 30 years inhaling and zero years exhaling. Grief and mourning and tears allowed me the complete exhalation of my spiritual lungs and the suffocation of the old man. Inhaling the life of Christ took very little effort after that.

For Discussion

1. Read John 14:15-27 and 1 John 2:1,2. Look at different translations and discuss the concept of the Paraklete.
2. What have you learned about Jesus in this chapter, particularly his ministry of comfort?
3. Discuss your thoughts on labeling emotions.
4. Have you ever experienced an extended period of mourning and grief? Would you be willing to discuss?
5. What needs to be exhaled in your life?

III

Blessed are the meek: for they shall inherit the earth

Blessed are the Mocked

If not the most well-known Beatitude, then assuredly the most well-scorned. Not many things that Jesus said have been subjected to centuries of such ridicule. In our present generation I cannot think of any statement more out of sync with our shared culture, whether politics, business or sports. Hyper self-promotion, trash talking, don't disrespect me, the arrogant pronouncements of certain future outcomes, the list is long. The thought of having meekness forced upon me, much less being proactively meek, is laughable.

Praus in Greek and *makkika* in Aramaic both generally translate humble and gentle. The Aramaic's lead meaning is to be low or lowliness. The verb translates to lower something. The Greek also implies what it is not. Meek is not harsh, rough, severe or cruel. So there you have it. No secret meanings that mean something else other than what it means. There is no getting around the extreme counter cultural finality of it all. Could I get a job with this quality? Can I compete in a win-at-all-costs world? Can I succeed at sports? Won't I get run over in every possible way? Can you imagine a future spouse attracted to your meekness? As much as I would like to extract some cool meaning out of the word Jesus used, that doesn't really mean what it means, there is no getting around it. He meant what he said. Meek is to be low, to be humble, to be gentle. To be meek ... aaaarghh!

Moreover, meekness is one of the famed nine fruit of the Spirit mentioned by Paul, against which there is no law. More about the "no law" later.

"But the fruit of the Spirit is love joy peace, patience, kindness, goodness, faithfulness, gentleness (*prautes*) and self-control. Against such there is there is no law." (Galatians 5:22,23 Greek in parentheses)

No way around it, we are stuck. However, what we can do is search for context. That is not to say that Jesus is telling us to be meek in some cases and others not. But we can find context.

The Land

Jesus quoted directly from the Psalms when offering this as one of his paths to happiness.

"A little while, and the wicked will be nor more; though you look for them, they will not be found. But the meek will inherit the land and enjoy great peace." (Psalm 37:10,11)

Notice that the NIV translates the Old Testament Hebrew as land but the New Testament Greek as earth, although the Aramaic word used by Jesus, *ar'ea*, and the Greek word used by Matthew, *ge*, could be translated earth or land. I don't dispute the translation of either for earth though I prefer the spirit of the Psalmist which prefers the land. Inheriting the land is something very personal, very destiny oriented, very purpose driven. Inheriting the earth sounds cool but not sure what it means. I suppose the Book of Revelation could give us some insight though it still seems impersonal to me. Try this on for size …

"Happy are the gentle, for they shall inherit their land."

Or,

"Happy are the gentle, for they shall inherit their destiny."

Now that is powerful! In fact, this seems so much more consistent with the present and future promise that is inherent in this promise of inheritance. I love this planet and want to be a good steward of its beauty and resources but if God chooses heaven, earth or some other planet as our eternal destination, I am good with that. However, I can very much see how inheriting our temporal and eternal destination that God has for us would be a real prospect for happiness.

Context

It is reasonable to search for context on this amazing standard from the very Psalm from which he quotes. Before we get verses 10 and 11, we have verses 3-9.

"Trust in the Lord and do good; dwell in the land (there is the land again) and enjoy safe pasture. Delight yourself in the Lord and he will give you the desires of your heart." (Psalm 37:3,4 parentheses mine)

Then the Psalmist transports us to the great courtroom in the sky.

"Commit your way to the Lord; trust in him and he will do this: He will make your righteousness shine like the dawn, the justice of your cause like the noonday sun. (Psalm 37:5,6)

The Septuagint translation of these two verses blows me away,

"Disclose your way to the Lord, and hope in him, and he will act. And he will publish your vindication like light, and your judgment like noonday." (NEV)

Then the Psalmist continues with how we should behave towards our earthly adversaries,

"Bridle your anger, trash your wrath, cool your pipes – it only makes things worse. Before long the crooks will be bankrupt; God-investors will soon own the store." (Psalm 37:8,9 TM)

The Psalmist finishes up,

"the wicked lie in wait for the righteous, seeking their very lives; but the Lord will not leave them in their power or let them be condemned when brought to trial." (Psalm 37:32,33)

The judicial context for gentleness and meekness is a clarion call. We make our case to the Lord, we seek our vindication from him, we want the judge to judge the justice of our cause and issue decrees on our behalf and against our true adversary. However, when it comes to our vindication with earthly adversaries then The Message says it best,

"Bridle your anger, trash your wrath, cool your pipes …"

Anger and wrath hinder the justice of God (James 1:20). Meekness accelerates the justice of God. As Paul says in Romans 12, give God space to work vengeance on your behalf. God's vengeance is a deeply satisfying vengeance. Our vengeance is anything but. Clearly, meekness in pursuit of justice against that which keeps us from fully possessing our destiny is called for. Possession of your land and those with whom God has entrusted you is what matters. Let's keep our eye on the prize. The subject of entering, conquering, and being fruitful in our granted inheritance is the object. Jesus is showing us the way.

No Law

In God's kingdom, within his legal economy, there is abundant legislation that has been passed on our behalf. It was and continues to be a democratic vote of three; Father, Son and Holy Spirit. This legislation and the issued decrees speak to our forgiveness, freedom, healing, peace, relationships, and destiny. It is incumbent upon us to work with our Chief Intercessor to face down the illegalities that assault these legislated graces, and more specifically, to not cradle things that inhibit the full execution of these amazing decrees. An urgent truth to know is that Father has empowered us with Holy Spirit to bring forth fruit against which there is no law (Galatians 5:23). These fruit are judicial graces that are now imputed to our new identity being formed in Christ. They are judicially granted and judicially empowered to withstand every illegality that assaults our new life and identity in Jesus. They are provided to us as a means rather than an end to accelerate our possession of the kingdom of God. If you are under the illusion that God's perfect timing always happens, then I don't know what to say. Like the stiff-necked ancient Hebrews I had my foot on the brakes for 20 years. I am thankful it wasn't the 40 year delay they experienced.

Ranked

We are not here to discuss all nine fruit mentioned, but to specifically focus on the one brought forth by Jesus in this beatitude. For so long we have focused on the "rock-star" fruit ... you know, love, joy and peace.

"But the fruit of the Spirit is love, joy, peace, forbearance, kindness, goodness, faithfulness, gentleness (*prautes*) and self-control." (Galatians 5:22 Greek in parentheses)

LAST! That is where I have historically ranked meekness and gentleness on the "fruit I desire" scale. I dig love and peace and joy and faithfulness. I know I need patience, kindness, goodness and self-control. But gentleness? Not even on my radar, when it should be preeminent in my pursuit and possession of God's destination for me.

Though we are anything but meek when it comes to the legal pursuit of our adversary and relentless accuser.

Revenge

We wrote earlier about vengeance, and without contradiction revenge and vengeance are related. Most cultures historically have some grudge ethic, but the ancients were particularly well regarded in this area. Possibly most well-known were the Greeks, who generally defined justice as "outdoing one's friends with good and one's enemies with harm." If you look at our modern choices, we might select the Sicilian mafia as the apotheosis of a revenge culture. Interestingly, the ancient Greeks colonized Sicily back in the 8th century BC, so the case could be made that the mafioso are really descended from the ancient Greeks. The guy on the cover of this book sure doesn't look meek.

The topic of revenge has spawned sayings that are delicious –

"Revenge is a dish best served cold."
-*Les Liaison Dangereuses*

"Revenge is a confession of pain."
-Latin Proverb

"Revenge is a kind of wild justice."
-Francis Bacon

"But if there is any further injury then you shall appoint as a penalty life for life, eye for eye, tooth for

tooth, hand for hand, foot for foot, burn for burn, wound for wound, bruise for bruise."
-Exodus 21:23-25

"I'm a fighter. I believe in the eye for an eye business. I'm no cheek turner. I got no respect for a man who won't hit back. You kill my dog, you better hide your cat."
-Muhammad Ali

"We should forgive our enemies, but not before they are hanged."
-Heinrich Heine

"Stronger than lover's love is lover's hate. Incurable, in each the wounds they make."
-Euripides

"To exact revenge for yourself or your friends is not only a right, it's an absolute duty."
-Stieg Larsson

"Funny thing about revenge. It could make a killer out of a nun."
-Kevis Hendrickson

"Revenge is sweet and not fattening."
-Alfred Hitchcock

"Never take your own revenge, beloved, but leave room for the wrath of God, for it is written, VENGEANCE IS MINE, I WILL REPAY, says the Lord."
-Romans 12:19

Christians have gotten into their minds that to desire vengeance is something deviant. To want revenge is really to want a certain justice. Listen to Jesus rebuke his disciples regarding their little faith –

"In a certain town there was a judge who neither feared God nor cared about men. And there was a widow in that town who kept coming to him with the plea, 'Grant me justice against my adversary.' For some time he refused, But finally he said to himself,

'Even though I don't fear God or care about men, yet because this widow keeps bothering me, I will see that she gets justice, so that she won't eventually wear me out with her coming!' And the Lord said, 'Listen to what the unjust judge says. And will not God bring about justice for his chosen ones, who cry out to him day and night? Will he keep putting them off? I tell you, he will see that they get justice, and quickly. However, when the Son of Man comes, will he find faith in the earth.'" (Luke 18:2-8)

This passage is famous for its emphasis on importunity. However, Jesus is very explicit on faith in the earth defined as perseverance in front of the great Judge. It is the constant crying for justice – for the granting of justice against our adversary.

That just doesn't feel like what we have so long been taught. Relentlessly crying out for vengeance, for justice, for restitution, for restoration. A without-ceasing and relentless pleading against our adversary, a continual coming to the judge, importunistically making a case. Even better, making a case for justice on behalf of our brothers and sisters in the Lord. Growing up in Jesus to be a junior advocate with our Senior Advocate - learning how to argue in the courtroom of heaven on behalf of those who don't yet know how. The prophet Jeremiah acknowledged two that were noted for making their arguments before the Most High. God was so frustrated with his nation that he said,

"Even if Moses and Samuel were to stand before me, my heart would not go out to this people." (Jeremiah 15:1)

What a compliment to Moses and Samuel to be considered advocates who could stand in the presence of the Lord and make a case for God's people.

Golf and the Kingdom

As a right-hander, if I swing outside-in to the left, the ball will go right; if I swing inside-out to the right, the ball will go left; If I swing down on the ball, it will go up; If I swing up at the ball; it will likely be a low grounder. What a crazy game!

The leaders serve, the servants lead; the humble are exalted, the exalted are humbled; the first shall be last and the last shall be first; the mighty are cast down from their thrones and those of low estate are lifted up; the hungry are filled with good things and the rich sent away empty; anger and revenge block the vengeance of God; meekness and gentleness accelerate God's justice. Moreover, meekness is the bridge over which our destiny moves from heaven and manifests in the earth.

Got that?

For Discussion

1. How do you react to the concept that meekness and gentleness are a path to happiness?
2. Do you agree with the author's contention that there is context for this Beatitude?
3. What does it mean to inherit the earth? Inherit the land? Inherit your destiny?
4. How is justice a part of the context for meekness in Psalm 37?
5. Jesus teaches that there are differences between God's kingdom and human kingdoms. Take time to discuss those differences.

IV

Blessed are they which do hunger and thirst after righteousness: for they shall be filled

Righteousness

On October 14, 1066 AD, the Battle of Hastings was fought between the Norman-French army of William the Duke of Normandy, and an English army led by the Anglo-Saxon King Harold. This battle marked the culmination of William's conquest of England. More importantly for us today, so began the French language invasion of the Old English tongue. The Germanic Anglo-Saxon language became deeply enriched with French and Latin vocabulary that has since made English one of the most versatile and expressive in the modern world. Our choices of words seem endless with multiple ways to say things with either French/Latin words or Anglo-Saxon words. One of those choices is the subject of this chapter and it is the translation of *dikaiosyne*, the Greek word for justice. *Dikaiosyne* is also famous for being one of the four great virtues of the ancient Greeks - justice, courage, prudence and temperance. Many of the philosophical writings and discussions of the ancients involved the virtue of justice. The undisputed preeminent work is *The Republic*, by Plato, a massive dialogue on the subject of justice whose concepts and quotes are relevant for today. The subject of *The Republic* was *dikaiosyne*. As you might expect, this virtue is a dominant theme in the New Testament. Notwithstanding, *dikaiosyne* is most often translated in the Bible using the English word righteousness rather than justice. For whatever reason our English translators preferred that word over the more historically accurate word *justice*. The Latin New Testament has *justitia*, the Spanish *justicia,* the French *justice*, but the English *righteousness*.

This brings us back to the Battle of Hastings. The word for *just* in Old English is *rihtwis* and in Old High German *rehtwisic.* They both mean the just way or the right way. *Rihtwis* became modern *righteous* and *rihtwisnes* became our modern *righteousness*. Translators are not stupid. Anglo-Saxon words move the native English-speaking soul; God, father, mother, brother, sister, house, dog, cat. What causes you to emote more ... to hear that someone is self-righteous or self-just. How about the "righteous wrath of God" or the "just wrath of God". I concede the Anglo-Saxon word moves me more. The point is that they are really the same word, we have a Germanic/Anglo-Saxon or a Latin/French word from which to choose. Certainly, over the years we have attributed different nuances of meaning to both words, but that doesn't change the fact that the translation of *dikaiosyne* is as much justice as it is righteousness. English translations of the Aramaic version rightly translate,

"Blessed are they which do hunger and thirst for justice (*kinuta*)."

My apologies for spending so much time making this case, but by translating this beatitude "righteousness," which emotes more, rather than "justice," which has more judicial-ness to it, we lose some of the power of what Christ was saying. Jesus is laying out a path to happiness, which is justice satisfied. If we pursue justice as we would pursue food and water, then we will be full and satisfied. Justice, full and satisfied, produces blessedness and happiness.

In my first book, *Our Father*, I wrote that Christians often struggle with the concept of justice because of how we are instructed by Jesus to respond to personal injustices. But to not be justice-minded is to conflate how we respond to injustice in the flesh and how we respond in the spirit, how we respond on the earth and how we respond in heaven. I won't repeat here the techniques used to pursue justice in heaven and in the spirit, but it should be stressed that to pursue it is a path to happiness.

Well Fed

"Filled," the Greek *chortazo*, to be well fed, satisfied, full. Being hungry and thirsty is not fun. Being well fed is. Think Thanksgiving Day, that is *chortazo*. So full, can't move or eat another bite, somehow the pumpkin pie made it down. Too much turkey, stuffing, potatoes, gravy, yeast rolls, green beans, squash, cranberry sauce, pumpkin pie, too much wine, plus football and family. That is *chortazo*. My favorite day of the year! Doesn't have the commercial pressure of Christmas, has the first hints of fall, all about satisfying relationships and food. A day of happiness for sure. It perfectly translates the Latin *satis-fied*. Enough done! *Satis* already.

Now imagine *chortazo* for the soul. Thoroughly, completely, utterly satiated. The Aramaic word that Jesus actually used has some hilarity to it. The word is *sb'e* and it defines very much like the Greek, to be sated or satiated. Moreover, it has the secondary meaning of "to be disgusted at," which makes sense since the idea is to be so filled up and full that you are disgusted. Have you ever been that full? I have. Again, Thanksgiving Day. I get so full I am absolutely miserable, so miserable that I would almost prefer to be hungry. Now that is full! Let's see if we have this right … when I hunger and thirst for justice, I will be filled up beyond the point of satisfaction to almost a state of discomfort because I am so full. So full it hurts. Disgustingly full. I can't help but chuckle at God's sense of humor.

Abundant Death

For many the abundant life in Christ is a rarity because we haven't first experienced abundant death.

"If anyone would come after me, he must deny (*arneomai*) himself and take up his cross daily and follow me." (Luke 9:23 Greek in parentheses)

We earlier read about the suffocation process to crucifixion. The word deny doesn't mean to deprive of personal pleasures and desires - it means so much more. It means to renounce and disown. We are to renounce and disown our self. But is there more than one self because Jesus says right after that,

"What good is it for a man to gain the whole world and lose or forfeit his very self?"

Are we just one self that is first renounced then gained or are we to renounce our false self and gain our true self? Or does it matter if there is a difference?

We also talked about the contradictions between the kingdom of heaven and the kingdoms of earth. On earth, the leaders lead, the servants serve, the first are first, the last are last, the proud and self-promoting are exalted, the humble are brought low, **you first live and then you die**. In heaven, the trades are flipped. The leaders serve, the servants lead, the first are last, the last are first, the proud are humbled, the humble are exalted, **you first die and then you live**.

"For whoever wants to save his life will lose it, but whoever loses his life for me will save it." (Luke 9:24)

As followers of Jesus, many of us have not yet truly learned to die. But you might say that the church today appears full of the walking dead, and I would agree. The church works hard to strip us of our desires and passions because they might lead to bad things. Then we next work hard at making our Christians nice people. Not courageous, or adventurous, or passionate, but really nice. Show me a follower of Jesus with an adventurous, passionate, robust, abundant life and I will show you a follow of Jesus who has learned to take up their cross daily.

"I have been crucified with Christ and I no longer live, but Christ lives in me. The life I live in the body, I live by the faith of the Son of God, who loved me and gave himself for me." (Galatians 2:20)

Evidently there are two I's here. The "I" that has been crucified and no longer lives and the "I" that is fused with Christ and lives by faith. Taking up our cross daily is the path to life. The true "I" cannot be formed and grow and until the false "I" is dead. The true "I" is received, and loved, and blessed, and chosen, and righteous, and pure, and courageous, and honored. The old, false "I" is cursed, and rejected, and despised, and sinful, and impure, and cowardly, and shamed. That old and false identity with its earthly DNA must be suffocated. At first it seems the crucifixion process is an endless battle. But if a zero-tolerance policy for the earthly schematics to rule over our heavenly schematics is imposed, the process becomes easier.

"Set your mind on things above, not on earthly things. For you died, and your life is now hidden with Christ in God." (Colossians 3:2,3)

In the letter to the Colossians, Paul takes crucifixion to a new level. More than by the Spirit putting to death the deeds of the flesh, it is further death to the basic principles that govern the kingdom of earth. This is radical thinking.

"Since you died with Christ to the basic principles of this world, why, as though you still belonged to it, do you submit to its rules?" (Colossians 2:20)

Then he ratchets it up even more with who you earthly are not,

"Here there is no Greek or Jew, circumcised or uncircumcised, barbarian, Scythian, slave or free, but Christ is all, and is in all." (Colossians 3:11)

You can choose to participate in this wild wind that is now blowing through the body of Christ and is even now breathing power into every organ, bone, limb, ligament and very marrow of which He is the head. This wind is sweeping away the earthly identities to which we attach so much hope and so much indignation, so much isolation, so much tribalism, so much victimizing, so much victimhood, so much pride and so much shame. This wind is filling the willing with the abundant life of Christ whose heavenly wiring is thoroughly available to all who believe.

Phaedo

After his sentence, Socrates' death was delayed because the annual sacred Athenian shipping mission to Delos had not yet returned. Finally, the overdue ship was spotted and the jailer informed Socrates that today would be the day he must drink the hemlock. Surrounded by his many friends and students they were able to have one last good argument, fittingly, about the immortality of the soul. Plato records this discussion and it comes to us titled *Phaedo*. Socrates makes three rational arguments for the soul's immortality and while doing so lays out concepts that would offer the dawn's light to the Apostle Paul's noon day sun on how to live.

"Did we not say some time ago that when the soul uses the instrumentality of the body for any inquiry, whether through sight or hearing or any other sense

– because using the body implies using the senses – it is drawn away by the body into the realm of the variable, and loses its way and becomes confused and dizzy, as though it were fuddled, through contact with things of a similar nature?"[10]

I hardly know where to start in dissecting this amazing approach to examination and inquiry. With great restraint I will confine my comments to the subject at hand and not go off on how deceiving the physical and sensate realm can be in the pursuit of truth. If our earthly schematics are so imperfect and deliverance at some level is possible while still operating in this body, would you be open to that?

"The truth is much more like this. If at its release the soul is pure and carries with it no contamination of the body, because it has never willingly associated with it in life, but has shunned it and kept itself separate as its regular practice – in other words, if it has pursued philosophy in the right way and really practiced how to face death easily – this is what 'practicing death' means, isn't it?"[11]

Practicing death? Taken in the context of the first excerpt, this is not so much asceticism as it is a denying of oneself, a renouncing and disowning of the earthly and mortal, an owning of the spiritual and immortal. That to do so is called practicing death in the Socratic tradition and taking up your cross in the Christian tradition. The theory of forms, to which the arguments of Phaedo are central, speak to the very core of the philosophic tradition in western civilization. Taking up one's cross speaks to the very heart of spiritual Christian tradition. And what does any of this have to do with the subject beatitude, to hunger and thirst for righteousness?

Spiritual Asthmatics

I have used breathing exercises for years, fully embracing their efficacy in the improvement of overall health. At first, as a beginning breather, I thought that inhaling deeply was foundational, you know, fill up your lungs by expanding first the lower diaphragm and then fill the upper part of the chest cavity. Then exhale and repeat. As I matured in my intentional exercises, I slowly learned that exhaling well was really the difficult part. A deep, purging, thorough exhale really took time, effort and discomfort. Then having exhaled well, inhaling deeply was rather easy. The air hunger created by exhaling well made filling up my lungs with rich oxygen a piece of cake. As I increased in knowledge and experience with these breathing exercises, I also added holding my breath to the list. But not just inhaling and holding my breath, rather seeing how long I could hold my breath after a long slow rich exhale, and to do it repeatedly. The carbon dioxide would build in my blood stream and in my body as I deprived myself of oxygen while holding my breath, or in this case, lack of breath. Finally, as the breath hunger grew the carbon dioxide would at last trigger an involuntary response to breathe and I would deeply gulp the precious air of life. There was no problem taking a deep drink of air. Later I learned that this is a popular breathing exercise for those with asthma, since asthma is not an inhalation problem but an exhalation problem. It is hard to inhale needed oxygen when the old air is still trapped in the lungs. Sounds like what someone being crucified might experience, at least from the point of breathing.

Too many followers of Jesus are spiritual asthmatics. The old used air is still trapped in our lungs and we cannot get it out. We try to breathe in new fresh air, but there is nowhere for the new air to go. The discomfort and effort required to empty our lungs is too much and we settle down to a level of shallow breathing as believers, with our favorite preachers and teachers serving as our steroidal inhalers when we get under stress. Then we go back to our shallow breathing, hoping to avoid conditions which activate a spiritual asthmatic attack that will again paralyze our spiritual breath.

Jesus proposed a life of hunger and thirst. Putting ourselves in a condition of absolute exhalation and emptiness, with all the associated discomfort until the emptiness triggers a gasping and gulping in the life and righteousness of Christ. Just like intentionally exhaling and holding my breath in that state of emptiness, feeling the air hunger grow, but still holding, until the holding is intolerable, and I must be filled and satisfied.

Kenosis

"Your attitude should the same as that of Christ Jesus: Who, being in very nature God, did not consider equality with God something to be grasped, but made himself nothing (*kenosis*), taking the very nature of a servant, being made in human likeness. And being found in appearance (*schemati*) as a man, he humbled himself and became obedient to death – even death on a cross!" (Philippians 2:5-8)

*Kenosis (*verb *keno-o)* literally translated means to make empty, to empty out. The kenosis of Christ is the emptying of himself, in this case, equality with God, the rights and privileges of his divinity, on which theologians are better equipped than I to elaborate. Suffice it to say that Christ emptied himself of some measure of his heavenly DNA and took on the very nature of a servant and the schematics and wiring of a man (*schemati* in the Greek). Humbling himself, he became obedient to death on a cross.

Now Christ asks us to do the same thing, but the opposite. It still requires humbling one's self and becoming obedient to death on a cross. Christ is asking us to empty ourselves of our earthly and human DNA and take on the very nature of a servant of God, being made in divine likeness. The death on the cross of our old earthly self requires considering our earthly genes, our earthly wiring and schematics, not something to be grasped, on the contrary, something of which we empty ourselves. This is the analogue for denying ourselves and taking up our cross daily. My earthly *schemati* is cast off and in the new birth I have received heavenly *schemati*. My heavenly *schemati* is now the true me, the true self, my true identity out of which every good fruit now has the possibility of abundance.

"Happy are those who take up their cross and fully empty themselves daily to the point of complete hunger and thirst for justice, for they will easily be filled and richly satisfied."

For Discussion

1. The concepts of justice and righteousness are combined in one Greek word. Discuss the different nuances of meaning we have given the two words in English.
2. Try and describe what the abundant life in Christ could be like. Discuss abundant death, especially in the context of your old self and new self.
3. Discuss spiritual asthma and what that means to you.
4. What is the kenosis of Christ? What is our kenosis?
5. How does kenosis help us understand what Jesus means when he uses the phrase "they which do hunger and thirst?"

V

Blessed are the merciful: for they shall obtain mercy

Mercy presents us with a semantic problem. The contemporary English word has a very restricted meaning, usually referring to an act of pardon or a reprieve from punishment. Mercy to an Anglophone implies the power to punish. Mercy is not so much what you get. It is what you don't get. The Greek word *eleos* used here by Matthew is a bit more expansive, translating also as loving-kindness or tender compassion. All these fit well judicially, especially when talking about the mercy of a judge or a court.

However, we are somewhat short-changed by these definitions, knowing that Jesus spoke Aramaic, a Semitic language, very close to Hebrew, much like

Italian is very close to Spanish. And we have an idea of the Aramaic word for mercy Jesus used here, *rachme*, similar in meaning to the Old Testament Hebrew *rachamim*. Are you ready? The primary meaning of *rachme* is 1) the womb; then 2) internal organs generally; then 3) sexual organs specifically; then like Greek 4) pity, mercy, favor; and finally, 5) love.

Human mercy that we have imputed to divinity as defined in western languages is pity, compassion, and an act of pardon or reprieve from punishment. As neat as that is it offers little in the way of divine judicial power, though it gives us a glimpse of the way humans view judicial power.

God made them in his own image, male and female. We call him Father, but he holds all the beauty given to a man and all the beauty given to a woman. Divine mercy is the awesome place and power of the feminine womb. The conception and birthplace of all that is new. There is no other human mercy that compares to a mother's mercy. To generalize, I wonder sometimes if many mothers even see any wrong in their child. She sees her children as they are supposed to be or truly are, not as they are acting out. If you want to see the closest thing to the Heavenly Father's mercy, look to the earthly Mother. Divine mercy gives birth, recreates, reinvents, all things are new, the old has passed away. Jesus said that you will know a tree by its fruit (Luke 6:45). The fruit of divine mercy is a new birth, a passing away of the old. It is like Isaiah said,

"Forget the former things; do not dwell on the past. See, I am doing a new thing! Now it springs up; do you not perceive it?" (43:18,19)

Mercy like destiny is a place - the birthplace of judicial power in the kingdom of God is in the womb of mercy. It is the location where the seed can find the egg and give hope to conception. Nothing sets the table for your liberty, your re-wiring, your reinvention, your re-coding of the genes, like this place of divine mercy. There is nothing else that provides you such a powerful judicial platform to cast aside the past in all its forms; to cast aside the enemy and all his chains that have held your family in bondage for generations. It does not flow from earth to heaven or from human to God. It can only flow from heaven to earth and from God to human. Read the rest of this verse from above –

"I am making a way in the desert and streams in the wasteland." (Isaiah 43:19)

The old way was a miracle path through the waters, the Red Sea, making the wet dry. The new way is a miracle path through the desert, making the dry wet. The old way was seeking power from earthly doing to heavenly being. The new way is bringing heavenly being to earthly doing, to be heavenly present and earthly empowered.

Without the womb of mercy there is no sustainable new way. Short-circuiting heavenly power for a tiny bowl of bitterness is a poor trade. Bitterness aborts the new person, the true you, the true self, birthed in Christ. There is no hope of creativity in bitterness.

Only the despair of becoming small-souled and exiled.

If I have not been clear, I will be so now. There is no new birth of any sort without the womb of mercy. If you cannot forgive yourself, forgive God, forgive your spouse, forgive your friends, forgive your enemies, forgive your parents, forgive whomever … THERE IS NO PATH FORWARD! The womb of mercy is the beginning point of all that is beautiful and enlarging, watching those amazing spiritual sonograms of seeing Christ formed in your true self.

Again, The Philosophers

The ancients would say that human love and the desire to procreate really come from the human desire for immortality. Plato describes the reason for love and desire in his *Symposium*.

"The mortal nature seeks to be ever existent and immortal. It can achieve this only in begetting, leaving a new creature behind in place of the old that passes away. This process of continual generations occurs, not only in the species, but also within the individual; for our bodies and those aspects of our souls associated with our bodies are continually dying. It is only for a little time that an animal is said to live and be the same, and even though he is called the same, he is not so, for he does not possess the same properties; the new is constantly replacing what is continually being lost. This applies not only to the body but to the soul; habits, customs, opinions, desires, pleasures, pains – all are continually changing. Even our knowledge is continually coming to be and passing away, so that we are never the same persons in what we know. Every mortal thing is preserved, not by remaining forever the same, but by substituting another like it for what departs. It is in this way that mortal nature has a share in immortality."[12]

This is some seriously advanced thinking in the 4th century BC and contemporary thinkers have done little to improve upon it. It just so happens that that Bible tells us how. Procreation between the divine and human spirit in the womb of mercy is the way to immortality and happiness.

"For God was pleased to have all his fulness dwell in him (Jesus), and through him to reconcile all things on earth or things in heaven, by making peace through his blood, shed on the cross." (Colossians 1:19,20 parentheses mine)

The reconciliation has happened. Yes, earth to earth and heaven to heaven, but more importantly heaven to earth. All things in heaven and all things on earth are reconciled, have now made peace, are now free flowing, are now trading partners and have traded ambassadors.

A Busted Marriage

I had been a pastor for almost eight years, the worst job on the planet ... well maybe not, but the worst job I ever had, and I have had some awful ones. I feel deeply for these men and women who serve as under-shepherds to the Great Shepherd. I learned the flock of God was not full of gentle lambs nor was I any prize as their pastor. While struggling to learn how to be a good leader and while in my last semester at college, half of my elders walked out and our church was in crisis. I was doing a Sunday evening series on marriage which was a complete joke since I was all of 26 years old. In addition to being a terrible pastor I was a terrible husband. I had a wife and two sons, so I guess that qualified me to opine on the subject. As a husband I was arrogant, domineering and verbally abusive. That my wife had not left me was a wonder, though I was to soon discover that she was considering it. After one of my Sunday evening messages teaching on the subject of marriage, we had come home and were settling down for the night. Unsurprisingly, we decided to launch into a discussion on the current state of our relationship. Like the clueless young man who had ignored years of obvious signals, I was shocked, stunned, incapacitated and many other emotions that were completely un-process-able in the moment. Avoiding the terrible details, suffice to say that we both utterly failed at mercy and forgiveness. My posing identity was inflamed and I could not figure out my way forward. Ultimately, I left the church, met a girl from Latin America and in my unstable mental state thought it would be a good idea to run off with her to South America. I remember signing the divorce papers in Caracas, Venezuela. Sometime later and somewhat like the prodigal son, I came to my senses and returned home, broke, broken, and more. My now ex-wife met me at the airport and we soon tried to make a go of reconciliation. Remarrying a year later we began the new journey of shut-down emotions and paying each other back for all the past inflicted hurts, for which mutual and utter contempt would be the final prize. I wouldn't want anyone to go through what we went through for the next 20 years, especially what I put her through. I considered our covenant irretrievably broken and could not find the place of mercy for me or for her. Then after twenty years my anger was finally exhausted, but now the damage inflicted on her, required her mercy, which was difficult in coming. It is hypocritical to think you can now forgive someone after you have paid them back ten-fold.

Finally, and fully like the prodigal son I came home. Thoroughly exhausted by anger, mostly towards God, and having squandered his inheritance for me, I spent two more years in letting Christ strip away the old identity that caused such destruction. Rejecting the old man was a daily, sometimes hourly process, but those two years largely began the process of tearing down what had been an unassailable fortress of falseness.

"The weapons of our warfare are not carnal, but mighty through God to the pulling down of fortresses" (2 Corinthians 10:4 my translation)

It was my dark night of the soul. At last I found the place of mercy, the mercy seat, the womb of mercy. The Christ-birthed identity, after all these years, began to form. My heavenly Father had forgiven me; my wife and family had forgiven me; and I had forgiven myself. Not finding the womb of mercy for oneself can often be the greatest battle of all.

Robots

When comparing our heavenly identity with our earth identity, I often hear the rebuttal that human nature is too full of beauty, variety and colorfulness. Why would we renounce our earthly self and put on our heavenly self? It all sounds very robotic. Indeed, are we all to be heavenly robots? My response to that is there is no greater panoply of gifts, personalities, callings, identities and destinies than can be found in the kingdom of heaven. On the contrary, human beings have a particular affinity for accumulating buttons all over their earthly selves. More amazingly, these buttons have titles on them so easily presented that people can press them with the most predictable outcomes. Peculiarly, those we are close to or care for the most can be particularly gifted at pressing our buttons, and we theirs. When these buttons are pressed the most expected responses then act out. Tell me now, who is the robot? I maintain that humans with all their buttons and humans who enjoy pushing those buttons are looked on by the angels as the closest thing to robots there can be.

Why not become button free?

"Honey, I know that you are behaving like a robot when you press my buttons and are looking for my robotic self to predictably respond (and my personality profile has confirmed it). But the robot is gone, in its place is my new self birthed in the womb of Christ's mercy. He has taken my buttons away. You can keep pressing but the wiring has changed."

I am not suggesting that you actually say this to the chief button pusher in your life, but at least you can think it.

For Discussion

1. Discuss the various definitions of mercy in the original languages, particularly the Aramaic meaning of the maternal womb.
2. What areas of your life need a reinvention and re-wiring?
3. Discuss the human desire for immortality, especially in the context of the creative process.
4. Where in your life do you need to find the place of mercy?
5. Describe some of the buttons on your self that people push.

VI

Blessed are the pure in heart: for they shall see God

Intimate or Inmate?

In times past I struggled with the quest for intimacy with God, with my wife and with friends, largely because I didn't know what it was. Many claim they want intimacy but don't know what it is, don't know when they have it, or if they think they have it, it is neither enough nor enduring. Thus trying to obtain that which was both unknowable and unachievable seemed like a wasted effort.

A friend and brother in Christ recently started a group discussion for men to pursue the subject of intimacy, with God primarily and our wives collaterally. At the time I considered a synonym for intimacy to be inmate and the pursuit of it a prison break with a ball and chain around my ankle. My challenge to the group was, "can we please spend time defining it before we go about discussing how to obtain it?" The very next meeting our little band was transported back in time as we engaged in a dialectical discussion of the definition of intimacy. The dialogue unfolded and just like the philosophical discussions of 2,500 years ago, we did a great job of refuting each other's presumptions without successfully landing on the truth. While having some *aporeia*, or perplexity, about what intimacy was, we generally agreed that it might be close to the following definition –

"To fully know and to be fully known."

Certainly, this is the promise held out to us by Paul in 1 Corinthians 13 that we will fully know as also we are already fully known. Fulfilling completely the promise of this kind of knowledge is probably not possible until the next life, however, that should not stop us in the meantime from the pursuit of fully knowing and being fully known. We may never gain perfection, but then again this life is not about that. Also, this very hesitant definition we came up with could easily be disputed by someone more skilled at dialectic discourse than we are. Regardless, for the plan of our little band of men and for the scheme of this discussion, let's build our case for now that intimacy is defined as such.

"Now we see but a poor reflection as in a mirror; then we shall see face to face. Now I know in part; then I shall know fully, even as I am fully known." (1 Corinthians 13:12)

Seeing and knowing, being seen and being known are couplets. To see God with total clarity, no impaired vision, no cataracts, is to know God ... fully. To see God is not only to know that we are already fully known by him but to know what his true knowledge of us is. This poses that we don't fully know ourselves and he knows us better than we do ourselves. And without dispute, God fully knows our newly birthed true self that many followers of Jesus are just now getting to see and know about themselves. To see the truth of who he really is and to see the truth of who we really are in his eyes is the beginning of intimacy. Jesus offers an illumined path for sustaining and growing this "seeing." But first to Diotima ...

Diotima

While instructing Socrates in the art of contemplation, Diotima, the female stranger from Mantineia offered on the role of "seeing."

"But what if man had eyes to see the true beauty – the divine beauty, I mean, pure and clear and unalloyed, not clogged with the pollutions of mortality and all the colors and vanities of human life – thither looking, and holding converse with the true beauty simple and divine? Remember how in that communion only, beholding beauty with the eye of the mind, he will be enabled to bring forth, not images of beauty, but realities (for he has hold not of an image but of reality), and bringing forth and nourishing true virtue to become the friend of God and be immortal, if mortal man may. Would that be an ignoble life?"[13]

Where do we begin with this guide on how to see the true beauty, the divine beauty? The goal is to commune and hold converse with the true one, seeing with the eye of the mind that one may bring forth not images but the real and true. I sense that the fruit of "seeing" has more to do with communion, truth and reality, than just an image.

Katharos

Pure in heart, or in the Greek, the *katharoi* in *kardias*.

Katharoi, or the singular *katharos*, surely translates here as pure, but better translates as clean and the verb *katharizo* to cleanse. Think about the English "catharsis," a cleansing. Being pure just sounds more holy and religious. When the Greek-speaking Jews spoke of the uncleanness related to breaking their law, they used the term *a-katharos*, unclean. When the New Testament speaks of unclean spirits, again the word used was *a-katharos*. The Greeks often used alphas on the front of their words to negativize them. When Jesus spoke of pruning the vine in John 15, John uses the word *katharizo*.

A pretty good rendering of this beatitude could go like this,

"Happy are the clean in heart because they shall have intimacy with God."

Or better yet,

"Happy are the clean in heart because they shall fully know God even as they are fully known by him."

All this talk begs the question then of what it means to be clean, or to be clean in heart. What is it of which we need to be cleansed? At the last supper Jesus gave us some insight on cleansing when he said,

"I am the true vine, and my Father is the gardener. He cuts off every branch in me that bears no fruit, while every branch that bears fruit he prunes (*katharizo*) so that it will be even more fruitful. You are already clean (*katharoi*) because of the word I have spoken to you." (John 15:1-3 parentheses mine)

Then later in the same discourse he says,

"Sanctify them by the truth; your word is truth." (John 17:17)

There must something about God's word, or more specifically, God's truth that is cleansing. Let's face it, there are few things more defiling than lies. When Isaiah spoke of the suffering of the coming Messiah he listed two specific virtues of this individual –

"... though he had done no violence, nor was any deceit in his mouth." (Isaiah 53:9)

Of all the things to emphasize in this coming savior, these were the two; he was not a man of violence nor a man of lies. He neither spoke them nor believed them. Truth, or lack of it, is a really, big deal. We have heard that being tempted doesn't mean that we are in sin. Like you, I have often wondered when the line between temptation and sin is crossed. Try this on for size,

"Woe to those who draw sin along with cords of deceit ..." (Isaiah 5:18)

It seems that deceit is the cord that attaches the wagon of sin to our horse. As soon as some deceit gets involved the line has been crossed. Truth and lies are everything. To receive and give truth is cleansing and to receive and give lies is defiling. Moreover, not just truth and lies told, but truth and lies believed. So let's expand this beatitude accordingly,

"Happy are those who allow truth to cleanse their hearts from lies believed, for they shall fully know God even as they are fully known by him."

Book of Truth

After the prophet Daniel had been fasting for three weeks the angel of the Lord came to visit him with extraordinary words.

"Do not be afraid, Daniel. Since the first day that you set your mind to gain understanding and to humble yourself before God, your words were heard, and I have come in response to them. But the prince of the Persian kingdom resisted me twenty-one days" (Daniel 10:12,13)

And then the angel says,

"Do you know why I have come to you? Soon I return to fight against the prince of Persia, and when I go, the prince of Greece will come; but first I will tell you what is written in the **Book of Truth.**" (Daniel 10:20,21 bold mine)

I am fascinated by the Book of Truth mentioned here. There must be a book in heaven that holds the truth of destinies of peoples and nations. What is revealed to Daniel is the destiny of his country for the next many centuries and ultimately to the end times.

My question is can we ourselves also gain access to this Book of Truth, or portions of it, about our destiny and any other thing that God allows us to see? Don't get me wrong, the Bible is my book of truth that has liberated my immortal soul while riding this mortal train. It is more than enough to usher me into the next life. But apparently there are scrolls in heaven and one is called the Book of Truth. If there exist in heaven scrolls of destinies, specific to our gifts and callings which are irrevocable, I wouldn't mind a peek. (Romans 11:29)

What is Truth?

So goes the famous question asked sarcastically by Pontius Pilate at Jesus' trial. Justice demands truth. If we demand justice, we must traffic in truth. The economy and machinery of God's kingdom is oiled by authenticity. Of course, it helps to always tell the truth and not traffic in deceit, but we more particularly speak of believing and receiving truth, of rejecting and renouncing lies, about who God is and who he has declared you to be. As said earlier, we cannot fully know as we are fully known unless we begin the process of rejecting the lies about who we think our Father in heaven is, especially if that knowledge has been poorly formed by our earthly experiences. Experiences are real, important and often educational, but they contribute little to nothing in telling us about who God is. No wonder we don't come close to fully knowing him, as long as we are chained to the lies that our enemy speaks to us. What we do and what is done to us are the two conduits that the kingdom of darkness primarily uses to invest in us hoping to receive a multiplied return.

Most believers would agree that at the head level of knowledge they are being accused, sometimes falsely, sometimes factually, often experientially, in the courtroom of heaven night and day (Revelation 12:12). What is lesser known is that God is also accused by spiritual wickedness to us. We are lied to about who God is by our adversary. These lies once received become agreements that we make about God, ourselves and others. These agreements then become powerful tools that are used to keep us on life's treadmill, going nowhere, never changing, daily leaking hope that things will ever be different, trapping us in earth-bound identities that emphasize blood, family, heritage, gender, sexuality, money, class, performance, education, job and titles. Hopelessness is the most common fruit of a planet-chained identity. Don't get me wrong, I very much identify with my family, to whom I am devoted, but it is also the DNA of this family that has gifted me a lot of crap to deal with and I have in turn passed it on to my children. I am now part of a new family.

"Now you are no longer strangers to God and foreigners to heaven, but you are members of God's very own family." (Ephesians 2:19 TLB)

"For this cause I bow my knees unto the Father of our Lord Jesus Christ, of whom the whole family in heaven and earth is named." (Ephesians 3:14,15 KJV)

Book of Lies

One morning I had arisen early to fellowship and hear from the Lord. Customarily I pull out my journal and begin to write down questions for him. Questions like,

"Jesus, would you tell me about yourself?"

"Jesus, what do you think about my heart, the true me?"

"Jesus, what do you think about the heart of my wife?"

"Jesus, what do you think about my children?"

"Jesus, do you have anything you want to say to me?"

"Jesus, would you show me how much you love me?"

Any many other such questions about my family, friends and others that are on my mind ... and then I begin to write what I hear the Lord saying to me. This particular morning, I was inquiring about the true me and the true heart of my family. I heard clearly and wrote,

"Make a list of the lies you tolerate about yourself and renounce them."

I was appalled at the thought of composing any document that had all the lies that my unseen accusers were charging me with or that I was condemning myself with. Having a list of truths made sense to me, but a list of lies? I reacted to this in much the same way that I reacted to negative feelings. To label them was to enable them. By falsely thinking that I was empowering the negative by acknowledging it, I had become emotionally shut down, afraid of anything negative. How much more do you think I reacted to the request that I write down the lies that had come against me and that I had made agreements with?

I couldn't do it, so I sat on these instructions doing nothing. A week later, I asked the same question and got this response,

"Yes, my son, I have something to say to you. Do not be afraid of the lies. Confront them. Face them. Challenge them. I reject these charges against you and your family, and so should you."

Hesitantly, I began to put together a book of lies. Like a sculptor, I was to chip away at that which was not the image of Christ in me and get to the true image. What happened next was one of the more transformative things I have ever done. I found myself picking up my little book randomly throughout the day and renouncing these lies about who I am and what is my destiny. I began renouncing false agreements that I had made about all things in heaven and earth. I began to cast down imaginations and every high thing that was exalting itself against the truths of God. Now, carrying the little book with me everywhere, I relish recording past agreements made that are contrary to God's plan for me and others for whom I pray, and reject them. The neuro-scientists are right. They are right because God is right. Labeling is not enabling. Quite the contrary. Labeling is disabling. What a revelation!

Nouns & Verbs

For decades I lived this relational cycle - I loved God; I tried valiantly to not sin and do right; I would fail; I would feel guilty and condemned by God; I would hide and avoid being relational with him; given enough time, I would come back and engage with my heavenly Father; Finally, I would start the cycle all over again. I wager that most Christians work a similar devotional rhythm. I spent a lot of time in

Romans believing that Paul's words in that book held the secret to success. But I couldn't find it. It always alluded me.

"For we know that our old self was crucified with him so that the body of sin might be done away with, that we should no longer be slaves to sin – because anyone who has died to sin has been freed from sin." (Romans 6:6)

That wasn't my experience! I didn't know how to crucify the old self and felt like a constant slave. Pure in heart? Are you kidding me? I had never resolved this immutable truth – that the words at Jesus' baptism were for me.

"You are my beloved son in whom I am well pleased."

My nouns were always defined by my verbs, not the other way around. I lied, therefore I was a liar. I cheated, therefore I was a cheater. I hated, therefore I was a hater. When it became clear to me that God uses nouns to begat verbs and Satan uses verbs to begat nouns, that my new heavenly identity is informed by nouns and my old earthly man is informed by verbs, I began to see the beauty of Paul's writings. Satan uses verbs to accuse with nouns. When I lied, he didn't announce that I lied, he announced that I was a liar! Satan's lies begin with verbs and he then uses those verbs to keep our old crucified-self revived with nouns. I do, therefore I am. Our heavenly Father, on the other hand, has resolved for us the nouns and adjectives that we are regardless of the verbs we do or have been done to us. God then wants verbs to proceed out of our nouns. I am therefore I do; not I do therefore I am. To some this may seem like semantics or a bunch of mental gymnastics, but that was the power and majesty of the gospel that Paul preached. No wonder, he was often accused of encouraging sin,

"Shall we go on sinning, so that grace may increase?" (Romans 6:1)

Paul was encouraging being, who we are in Christ, all the nouns and adjectives that are truth about our new identity, regardless of the contrary verbs that are still manifesting in our behavior. When our accuser tries to take one of those bad verbs and turn it into a bad noun, that is the battle ground. Allowing the rich and beautiful nouns of the new creation inside us to be fully embraced will eventually manifest positive verbs in our life and we can become fruitful lovers of God.

For Discussion

1. The author suggests that intimacy is defined as fully knowing and being fully known. What is your definition?
2. Read Ephesians 1:15-21. How are seeing and knowing related?
3. Discuss the New Testament Greek word for pure.
4. What lies do you believe about yourself? What lies do you believe about God?
5. Discuss the concepts of nouns and verbs.

VII

Blessed are the peacemakers: for they shall be called the children of God

Shlama

Speaking in his native Aramaic, the powerful and expressive lingua franca of three successive empires, Jesus said,

"Happy are the makers of peace (*shlama*)"

Hebrew had become the religious language of the scriptures and synagogue only and was on its way to dying out as an actively spoken tongue. Had Jesus said this in Hebrew, he would have said,

"Happy are the makers of peace (*shalom*)."

What is a maker of *shlama* or a *shlama*-maker? The younger brother of Jesus gives us some insight when he writes,

"Peacemakers who sow in peace reap a harvest of righteousness (justice)." (James 3:18 parentheses mine)

Shlama-makers sow seeds of peace which produce a harvest of justice. So we see that unsurprisingly this beatitude is deeply linked to the cause of justice. This refrain continues with Paul when he writes that the old legal system is a barrier and dividing wall of hostility between people and the only way to make peace is to put to death through the cross the hostile wall of human performance and cultural identity.

"For he himself is our peace, who has made the two one and has destroyed the barrier, the dividing wall of hostility, by abolishing in his flesh the law and its commandments and regulations. His purpose was to create in himself one new man out of two, thus making peace, and in this one body to reconcile both of them through the cross, by which he put to death their hostility." (Ephesians 2:14-16)

We now see further that the definition of a *shlama*-maker is to make two into one, to reconcile. Jesus' purpose as the ultimate peacemaker is to create in himself one new person out of two, thus making peace. The dividing wall is a legal system based on performance, based on successful doing versus a legal system built upon the birthed identity of God in us. Few things divide like a justice system predicated upon performance. We have it, we live in it and, so long as we have fallen humanity, it will at a certain level be necessary to function. In the movie *The Matrix*, humans are trapped in a false reality with enforcers that put down any attempt to throw off the un-reality. Neo, somewhat like Jesus, comes to throw off the chains of the old, defeat the enforcers and show the way out. Paul is advocating that the dividing wall of hostility is a complete legal infrastructure predicated upon performance that produces posing identities of false selves. The harvest of a new justice system built on the cross of Christ is not only capable of removing that barrier but uniting two into one at an identity level.

"Therefore, if anyone is in Christ, he is a new creation; the old has gone, the new has come! All this is from God, who reconciled us to himself through Christ and gave us the ministry of reconciliation." (2 Corinthians 5:17,18)

What does making one, or making peace, or making *shlama* mean? It means that we share genetic code, we share spiritual DNA, we partake from the same heavenly genome, we share the same ...

Family

Before digging in on this, let's get right to the punch line. Next to the Father and his first-born, there is no greater place of authority than being a child and an heir.

"Yet to all who received him, to those who believed in his name, he gave the right to become children of God – children born not of natural descent, nor of human decision or a husband's will, but born of God." (John 1:12,13)

The constant affirmation of our true son-ship and daughter-ship in heaven and so on earth is the final say on everything.

Accuser: "Did you see what he did?"

Father: "He is my son."

Accuser: "Did you hear what she said?"

Father: "She is my daughter."

Knowing this, Jesus states that maximizing the judicial authority as an heir of God proceeds out of a place of peacemaking.

There can possibly be no greater happiness to obtain than at last resolving our identity. This new identity is not some allegory or some metaphor but involves a real regeneration of the human spirit that can re-wire and re-train the brain, and some would say affect even our bodies.

So I ask you, though it may be a source of pride or disgrace, do you draw your identity from natural descent? From human decision? From your parent's will? From human acceptance or rejection? From human nurture or abuse? As important and impactful as all of these are, there is no deep abiding happiness that comes from it. That is the price of fallible human DNA, the price of imperfection. We must draw our identity from our new spiritual chromosomes that are now the core of our being and, moreover, have the power to neutralize the human heredity that has kept us earth bound and unempowered.

Resolving daily that we are children of the Father reaches far. Jesus knew the real deal even when he was 12 years old,

"Didn't you know I had to be in my Father's house." (Luke 2;49)

The Dividing Wall

Paul called the law, the commandments and the regulations a dividing wall of hostility (Ephesians 2:14-16). Timothy Keller comments on a recent debate,

"Recently, a 'new perspective' has developed over what the term 'works of the law' means. Many interpreters believe Paul is talking about the Mosaic ceremonial law only – circumcision, the dietary laws, the other laws which are about keeping ritually 'clean'. In this view, 'works of the law' is not moral performance in general, but the adoption of Jewish cultural customs and ethnic boundary markers ... So in this 'new perspective' the Judaizers are not legalists, but nationalists. And Paul is therefore not opposing salvation-by-works, but rather racial and ethnic exclusivity ... You cannot drive a wedge between nationalism and legalism as if they are two separate things ... But nationalism is legalism. Legalism is adding *anything* to Jesus Christ as a requirement for full acceptance with God. A moral superiority that comes from good works or from racial and cultural pedigree grows out of the same spiritual root." [14]

Whether moral performance or racial and cultural identity, both are dividing walls of hostility into which we are called to be ambassadors of reconciliation. There is only one true answer that destroys those walls and it is the cross of Christ. Followers of Jesus are told to renounce their false "selves" and take up their crosses daily, and so gain their true "selves." This is the beginning of peacemaking.

Called

"They shall be called the children of God."

Some questions ... called a child of God by whom and to whom? How? Where?

"Because those who are led by the Spirit of God are the sons of God. For you did not received the spirit that makes you a slave again to fear, but you received the Spirit of sonship. And by him we cry, 'Abba, Father.' The Spirit himself testifies (*sym-martyreo*) with our spirit that we are God's children." (Romans 8:14-16)

This is such an interesting passage. *Sym* in the Greek means together with. *Martyreo* means to testify or to be a witness, think martyr, particularly in a courtroom. The Holy Spirit is not just testifying to our spirit that we are God's children, the Holy Spirit is testifying with our spirit to something or someone else. It is important that we are continually affirmed by God of our family status, but it is also important that the enemy of that family relationship is testified against. Notice how *sym* is involved though. The Holy Spirit doesn't do it alone, we must be involved together in testifying that we are God's children against the specious argument that there is no possible way our thoughts and behaviors could agree with that. When our heavenly identity is under such assault and we find ourselves succumbing to our earthly selfness, then even provision is made there. A few verses later,

"Likewise the Spirit helps us in our weakness. For we do not know what to pray for as we ought, but the Spirit himself intercedes for us with groanings too deep for words." (Romans 8:26)

If we are unable to do anything else other than place ourselves in a position to be regularly affirmed that God is our Father and we are his child, then we have a shot.

Genealogy

The nature vs. nurture argument has no end in sight. Sitting next to my grandfather at his 90th birthday celebration, he leaned over and whispered in my ear,

"Remember that it is all in the genes."

From a man who raised cattle and hogs in northwest Missouri, this was his conclusion. There was little debate. He was very proud of his human heritage and had passed along that pride to his children. He was a very involved father to my mother and her two siblings, but I don't think any of them enjoyed his style of nurturing. His was a tough hand from farm land. He may have believed even then that human genetic coding was going to win the day anyway.

Mom came from a rural town, population about 500 and Dad came from a town 12 miles away, population about half that. These families were hardworking mid-westerners, proud of their work ethic, proud to be midwestern Americans, not quite poor, but proud. They were families of the earth, deeply bound to the land. Dad was the first one to go to college and that was because of a baseball scholarship. My brother, sister and I were the first to be raised in a city. Many generations on both sides of my family are buried in one small county in northwest Missouri, and most in one small town cemetery. My great, great grandparents on down. My grandfathers lived long lives, one died at 90 and the other at 92. I had the great privilege of being close to all my grandparents, spending every summer on the farm, working hard, eating large and going to sleep every night exhausted. Though a city boy, I fell in love with the land, saw the hardships and vagaries of farming. At 14 years old I was driving heavy farm equipment, often on the main roads to move them from farm to farm. I loved my grandparents and was very proud of them. I loved my hardworking Mom and Dad and was very proud of them. They all set a standard of character that was almost impossible to live up to.

We are all raised with advantages and disadvantages. I didn't have the advantage of a family that had a history of education or money. I did have the advantage of having a family that loved and were close and held a deep system of values that guided their choices. Willfulness and stubbornness seemed required to survive and thrive in tough conditions. I was very proud of my family. Very proud of my genealogy. Though our grandparents have been gone for some time, the rest of us remain very close and committed to this day. My earthly heritage is full of powerful blessings and curses and it has been no easy feat to allow the heavenly schematics of Christ to be formed. Both the pride and shame of heritage work their dark magic to quench the light.

My wife has the opposite story. She never knew her grandparents on either side of the family. Her maternal grandparents emigrated from Italy and settled in Boston. Her grandfather soon lost his wife and his leg. I don't think the two losses were related, but both rendered him unable to care for the youngest, my wife's mother, so he put her into a home for Italian children, where she spent many years being raised until he could bring her back home. By then he had remarried a step-monster and living at the Italian home for children didn't look so bad. My wife's mom brought all that damage of rejection into her adult life and passed it on. My wife has now become a case study on how one can get set free from her genealogy. Interestingly, that she has largely been set free from her earthly heritage has facilitated her ability to continue in relationship with her mother. Rejecting a genetic relationship does not mean one is free from the heredity of the flesh or from the genome of the family soul.

Melchizedek

Genesis 14 makes a beautiful link between justice and peace when Abraham returns from defeating a host of kings in battle. Melchizedek King of Salem, priest of the most-high God, comes out to meet Abraham and bless him. Melchizedek King of Salem literally translated means King of justice, King of peace. Need more be said? The priest was a king of justice and peace. (Hebrews 7:1,2)

1,000 years later King David comes along and prophecies that Messiah would come and be a priest forever after the order of Melchizedek. (Psalm 110:4)

The Christ would be a Priest who is both a King of Peace and a King of Justice. Furthermore, great emphasis was placed on Melchizedek's lack of ancestry as compared to a priesthood that emphasized geneaology.

"Without father or mother, without beginning of days or end of life, like the Son of God, he remains a priest forever." (Hebrews 7:3)

"And what we have said is even more clear if another priest like Melchizedek appears, one who has become a priest not on the basis of a regulation as to his ancestry but on the basis of the power of an indestructible life. For it is declared: 'You are a priest forever, in the order of Melchizedek.'" (Hebrews 7:15-17)

There is no more powerful example of the judicial authority for reconciliation that proceeds out of peacemaking than the repudiation of ancestral regulation and operating in the power of the indestructible life that is now our new inner nature received from Christ. How awesome it is to consider that Jesus paved the way with a powerful priesthood whose very efficacy is defined by its throwing off the shackles of earthly ancestry and defeating the destructions of the adversary with a life defined as indestructible.

Peace Beer

In many languages, English excepted, make and do are the same word. So it is in Greek, which says peace-maker or peace-doer. In the Aramaic it is maker of peace or doer of peace. The Greek word for peace is *eirene*, where we get our English female name Irene. The Aramaic *shlama* and the Hebrew *shalom* have even larger meanings. The primary meaning is "to be whole" or "to live well." Next come reconciliation and harmony between two parties and lastly comes victory over one's enemies. The New Testament Greek *eirene* was heavily influenced by its Aramaic and Hebraic sources. Used often in greetings and farewells as a blessing it is translated "May your life be filled with health, prosperity and victory." [15]

But wholeness and the integrity of our being are foremost at the heart of *shlama*. One of the things we learn from Paul is that **doing is not doable, nor is making makeable.** Being is doable and makeable and gives possibility to doing and making. So it is with peace. It is not possible to be a peacemaker without being a peace be-er. The power to make peace proceeds from the place of peace.

In John 14 Jesus reveals that there is an earthly peace and a heavenly peace. While our hearts can be troubled both by the dysfunctional old person and by external circumstances, the objective is not to be removed from trouble and fear but to move into peace. King David had tapped into this principle. There were few men more troubled than he was. His approach to trouble and fear was location and geography, a place.

"The Lord is my light and my salvation – whom shall I fear? The Lord is the stronghold of my life – of whom shall I be afraid? When evil men advance against me to devour my flesh, when my enemies and my foes attack me, they will stumble and fall. Though an army besiege me, my heart will not fear; though war break out against me, even then will I be confident." (Psalm 27:1-3)

What was David's secret? Just one thing …

"One thing I ask of the Lord, this is what I seek: that I may dwell in the house of the Lord all the days of my life, to gaze upon the beauty of the Lord and to seek him in his temple. For in the day of trouble he will keep me safe in his dwelling; he will hide me in the shelter of his tabernacle and set me high upon a rock. Then my head will be exalted above the enemies who surround me." (Psalm 27:4-6)

The Lord called David a man after his own heart. Even the name David means "Beloved." This deeply flawed man had figured it out. The secret to peace was location. To be in God's presence always and to gaze upon his beauty. We think Plato had tapped into something new when he wrote about gazing upon the heavenly beauty, but here we have David writing about this six centuries earlier. To be present in God's place for us is to possess God's peace for us.

As Paul said, let the peace of Christ rule as the judicial authority (*brabeuo*) in your heart (Colossians 3:15). It is the manifestation that you are right where the Father wants you.

Peace isn't some passive feeling and is more than just a preventive and prescriptive for being troubled and afraid. It is a fruit of the Holy Spirit that is a combination of identity and location. Resolving who you are in Christ can be a violent and daily process.

Taking the land even sounds war-like. **But power proceeds from a place of peace.** Like being loved jump starts my being a lover, so being in the place of peace empowers my peacemaking.

For Discussion

1. According to this book, peacemaking is defined as reconciling two into one. What is your definition?
2. What does being in the family of God mean to you? Your position and place? Your rights? Your rebirth?
3. What is the dividing wall of hostility?
4. What is the role of the Holy Spirit relative to this Beatitude?
5. What are some of the blessings and curses of your genealogy that you deal with?

VIII

Blessed are they which are persecuted for righteousness' sake: for theirs is the kingdom of heaven

For Justice's Sake

And the rest of this particular Beatitude –

"Blessed are you when people insult you, persecute you and falsely say all kinds of evil against you because of me. Rejoice and be glad, because great is your reward in heaven, for in the same way they persecuted the prophets who were before you." (Matthew 5:11,12)

Listen to Jeremiah in the courtroom of the Lord,

"O Lord, you took up my case; you redeemed my life. You have seen, O Lord, the wrong done to me. Uphold my cause! You have seen the depth of their vengeance, all their plots against me. O Lord, you have heard their insults, all their plots against me – what my enemies whisper and mutter against me all day long." (Lamentations 3:58-62)

Happy are those who are persecuted for the cause of justice (*dikaiosyne*) for the kingdom of heaven is theirs.

Or,

Happy are those who are persecuted when they prosecute injustice for the kingdom of heaven is theirs.

Jesus wraps this up with the nut of it all. The cause of justice is what it is all about. What is it? It is happiness. There is not much happiness to be found in injustice. There is little happiness to be found in isolating yourself to avoid the cause. You will be not be persecuted for the cause of justice if you are not prosecuting the cause of justice. Prosecution and persecution will go hand in hand. Injustice fights back, it is a worthy opponent, so worthy that often injustice on earth is temporarily victorious.

Whatever our destiny of prosecuting injustice on earth looks like, we all are called to prosecute injustice in our Heavenly Father's courtroom. Again, you will not likely be persecuted for the cause of justice if you haven't prosecuted for the cause of justice!

"Is not this the kind of fasting I have chosen: to loose the chains of injustice and untie the cords of the yoke, to set the oppressed free and to break every yoke." (Isaiah 58:6)

Prosecuting injustice takes courage. It may not end well. The greatest ancient voices against injustice were the Hebrew prophets who fearlessly spoke truth to power and largely suffered the consequences. I am humored by the sometimes consequence free fearlessness of today's truth-to-power speakers, in America anyway. Here we often celebrate truth-to-power speaking. Regarding those ancient prophets - as amazing as were their judgments flashing like lightening upon the perps, their prosecutorial behavior before God was even more so. And that is the type of transaction with our Father in heaven that is the subject of this book.

The Roman Road

"The book of Romans is the most sustained explanation of the heart of the gospel, and the most thrilling exploration of how that gospel goes to work in our hearts."[13]

Even a casual reading of this extraordinary letter tantalizes the soul with not only salvation, but also the abundant life. The first seven chapters answer the question what; what is salvation by faith? What is union with Christ? It is an ascent to the mountain top of hope for our spirit and an equally breathtaking descent into despair for our flesh, blowing the gap wide open at the end of chapter 7 ...

"For in my inner being I delight in God's law; but I see another law at work in the members of my body, waging war against the law of my mind and making me a prisoner of the law of sin at work in my members. What a wretched man I am! Who will rescue me from this body of death? Thanks be to God – through Jesus Christ our Lord!" (Romans 7:22-25)

Then come chapters 8-16, answering the question of how faith in Christ leads to real change. I had always known that these amazing words had victory all over them, but I couldn't crack the code. The majesty of chapter 8 suggested to me that the truth packed in there was it, but I was like one with a map to the treasure and still couldn't find the X. The revolution of my prayer life began with the revelation of my active role in the advocacy of Jesus Christ and the Holy Spirit on my behalf and on behalf of all those for whom I approach the heavenly Judge's bench. Seeking, indeed demanding, justice before God, obtaining his verdicts in heaven, carrying them boldly as his truth and now my truth, and expecting them to be imposed upon my reality on earth are all my earnest expectation. Almost all on earth and even some in the heavenlies conspire to convince us that we are children of the earth more than we are children of God. Our heavenly child-ness is the very first justice that requires irrevocable resolution.

This verse from Romans used in the previous chapter is worth repeating, it is that important. I was taught the three parts to a great presentation are 1) Tell them what you are going to tell them, 2) Tell them, 3) Tell them what you told them. So let's repeat,

"For you did not receive a spirit that makes you a slave again to fear, but you received the Spirit of sonship. And by him we cry, 'Abba, Father.' The

Spirit himself testifies with (*sym-martyreo*) our spirit that we are God's children." (Romans 8:15,16)

I hope you enjoy our occasional exegetical excursions and this is one worth taking. Greek prepositions are often used in combination with verbs or nouns to add specific or intensive meaning. The preposition *sym*, sometimes *syn* or *syng* in composition, mostly translates "together with." The beautiful verse is worth parsing to more fully understand the legal transaction that is taking place. From the previous chapter, the Greek tells us not just that the Spirit is testifying to our spirit, but that the Spirit is testifying together with our spirit. To whom are we jointly giving testimony? Our spirit and Holy Spirit together advocating against forces in heaven and on earth that complain to the contrary! Furthermore, with slavery as the ultimate injustice and liberty the ultimate justice, resolving our immortal sonship is the beginning of all liberty and the predicate for our prosecutorial boldness.

Note the very next verse,

"Now if we are God's children, then we are heirs of God and co-heirs (*syng-kleronmoi*) with Christ, if indeed we share (*sym-paschomen*) in his sufferings in order that we also share (*sym-doksasthomen*) in his glory." (Romans 8:17 parentheses mine)

In a matter of three verses *sym* or its variant is used four times, translated consecutively as "with," "co-" and "share" twice. I really like the use of co- by the NIV. If in the subject verse we used co-, it would go like this,

"The Spirit himself co-testifies with our spirit that we are God's children."

Justice Warriors

If we are to love our neighbors as ourselves then that suggests self-wellness is the foundation to bringing wellness to others. Self-justice is the foundation to bringing justice to others. To prosecute injustice for others first requires putting the oxygen mask on ourselves. We have enough witnesses witnessing to things not being lived out in their own lives. We need the mighty legal testimony of those who are not tolerating the illegal and unjust in their own world and can show us the way.

How self-well must I be to be an effective justice warrior for Christ? Have I yet worn you out with the refrain - resolving that we are children of the Father is the place of beginning? That God is our good Father and we are his beloved children is the first legal transaction that has to be judicially enforced.

Paul often says that we have been adopted by the Father (Romans 8, Galatians 4, Ephesians 1). Adoption might suggest that we are children in name only and not genetically imbued with the heavenly DNA of our maker, but that would be to misinterpret what Paul is saying. Though being a child of the Father in name only is powerful enough, there are too many passages that speak to our new birth, new heart, new spirit and new mind. What the Apostle means by the term adoption is that our standing as children has been legally and judicially gained. It is the first enforcement action required and the first right that Satan will try and illegally move us off of. Circumstances, things we have done and things done to us all conspire against our solid identity as a child in the family of heaven. In pursuit of justice on behalf of those to whom God has sent us, it is the first justice for which we ought to fight. According to Romans 8 the revelation of the children of God is the earnest expectation of all creation. Heaven and earth are crying out for the children of God to be revealed as the children of the Father, the children of inheritance, the children of victory, the children who take their legal place in the family, children with an eternal genome, children full of the Holy Spirit which is the down payment of our future glory.

When we are resolved that we are sons and daughters in the family of our Father and enforce that licit right, all hell will break loose. Every attempt to move you will be made. Let the persecution begin. If the authority of darkness can impose its phoniness on your rock-solid place in the kingdom of light, into which you have been metastasized (sounds cellular to me), then all hope for the construction of a justice warrior is lost!

"Giving thanks to the Father, who has qualified you to share in the inheritance of the saints in the kingdom of light. For he has rescued us from the dominion of darkness and brought (*metestesen = metastasized*) us into the kingdom of the son he loves." (Colossians 1:12,13 Greek in parentheses)

Don't for a minute not think that what has a legally happened to you as a believer and follower of Jesus is anything less than cellular in more ways than you and I can imagine.

"He was in the world, and though the world was made through him, the world did not recognize him. He came to that which was his own, but his own did not receive him. Yet to all who received him, to those who believed in his name, he gave the right to become children of God – children born not of natural descent, nor of human decision or a husband's will, but born of God." (John 1:10-13)

Let's re-phrase this beatitude to appropriately say,

"Happy are they which are persecuted for the sake of prosecuting injustice, for theirs is the kingdom of heaven."

For Discussion

1. What are some causes for justice that you are passionate about?
2. Read Luke 18:1-8. Discuss the concept of pleading for justice and prosecuting injustice before God.
3. How does this work with being present in heaven and empowered on earth?
4. What is the first thing required to be a justice warrior?
5. What is the first justice that the author maintains should be pursued?

IX

Conclusion

Working Theories

"It is our duty to do one of two things, either to ascertain the facts, whether by seeking instruction or by personal discovery, or, if this is impossible, to select the best and most dependable theory which human intelligence can supply, and use it as a raft to ride the seas of life – that is, assuming that we cannot make our journey with greater confidence and security by the surer means of a divine revelation."[16]

So Simmias responded to Socrates on the last day's discussion.

In past times Christianity's powerful case to the world typically had existing posts on which to build, such as belief in God generally, or in an after life, or in sin or wrongdoing. Today's growing secular world doesn't believe in a God, nor in an afterlife, nor in sin, nor in absolute truth, since the only truth is an individual's own personal reality.

According to Timothy Keller, the primary way to challenge a secularist is to question them about their working theories on 1) how to find meaning in life, 2) how to handle suffering, 3) how to find contentment, satisfaction and a happy life, 4) how to have a strong and solid identity, and 5) a basis for doing justice.

On most of these the secular apologist will come up empty. Secular resources just don't provide a lot of help in developing working theories for many of the above. The gospel of Jesus Christ arguably provides the best ideas to do just that. Moreover, it can be contended that specifically the Beatitudes speak directly to each of these things. To some, that doesn't prove that the message of Jesus is true, but they won't dispute that wouldn't it be great if it were true.

Pursuant to Simmias, the best and most dependable theory to use as a raft to ride the seas of life is selected by either seeking instruction, personal discovery, or best of all, divine revelation.

I was sinking and drowning with few answers and fewer theories. Certainly, none related to the five previous questions posed. After coming to complete intellectual and spiritual bankruptcy, I chose to have a life raft constructed that answered all five questions. Coming to Christ was easy. Having Christ formed in me, not so much. But why should I resist what works?

Epilogue

These first two books in our series on judicial power have explored deeply the concepts of destiny and identity, as offered by Jesus Christ. For certain, the uncomfortable concepts of enemies, lies, vengeance, warfare, courtroom hostilities and other such have possibly upended your gentle faith. I understand. We live in a violent world. Nature itself can be the most violent of all, though nature would respond that it is just nature. I marvel often, looking closely at the ground and observng the violence that the small creatures of this planet inflict on each other. Even beyond our earth, the birth and growth of galaxies in all their beauty and glory is nothing if not violent. What makes the New Testament so unique is its approach to bifurcating how one behaves in the physical versus how one operates in the spirit. We are gentle and meek to our earthly companions and adversaries, while concurrently bringing enormous violence to bear against our spiritual adversaries. Learning to be spiritual warriors in Christ, or better said, spiritual lawyers is the design. Injustice has no mercy. Becoming a true justice warrior requires spiritual backbone. Let us become brave servants in the Kingdom of Heaven who can press the legislated justices of the cross on behalf of ourselves and those who don't yet know how.

Admittedly, I have spent space telling you what to do without much on how to do it. That might be more the subject of another book, but I will start you here with a hint. How do I pray regarding my spiritual adversaries and enemies? What does that sound like? How is an argument in the courtroom of heaven against the accuser's lies composed? Shan, you are advocating for spiritual violence against injustice and its spiritual progenitors. How do I begin?

I am endlessly entertained by presentations that offer the 10 steps to this, or the five keys to that, or the two secrets to … well, you get my point. But having said that, I will share with you a secret. The Book of Psalms may be the most beloved prayer book in the world. Over half the Psalms were written by King

David, the most famous warrior in Israel's history. Because David was such a violent and bloody man God would not let him build the temple, yet of all people, David was a man after God's own heart. More than half of the Psalms written by David cry out to God against his enemies and the enemies of the nation. Some are downright imprecatory, so imprecatory that they feel un-Christian, unreadable and un-pray-able. Many who love the Psalms skip over these rich prayers because they don't fit well with how we have been taught a follower of Jesus is to think and believe. What we miss is how these violent prayers and arguments translate so articulately into a heavenly courtroom against a spiritual enemy. They are powerful and can begin to give you a voice before the great Judge.

Coda

The very talented son of some close friends had been on a spiritual odyssey. Thinking that taking a religion survey course at college seemed like a good way to begin, he came to me and asked my opinion. I couldn't help offering him my own three-hour religion survey course and summed it up in a letter that I left with him. Personally, I see the beauty in most faiths. They have appeal for many different reasons and have an efficacy to them that produces results, albeit, different results. The letter that I left with him some would no doubt find offensive, for it is impossible to sum any faith in a paragraph or two. I understand that and would accept challenges to my effort without contradiction. I tried in short form to show him the beauty, appeal and effectiveness of each.

Dear Matthew,

The birthplace for life, success and the pursuit of happiness for all of us is

FAILURE, SHAME & SUFFERING

Until we get there, the journey cannot really begin ... Through the millennia, however, humans have acknowledged that to remain in that state imprisons the human spirit, fostering hopelessness. Though there are multiple solutions that speak to this human condition, they seem to be generally summed up into three categories –

a) Desire and attachment are the causes of failure, shame, dissatisfaction and suffering. Work on a self identity that desires less and is not attached – Buddha, Stoicism. Can be very effective but will always have limited appeal. The human heart just desires too greatly.

b) Performance and achievement, a self identity that believes **I do therefore I am** – Moses, Muhammed, and most cultures on earth. These cultures and belief systems are heavy on laws, rules and regulations. They are very popular and will likely always be in the majority because they provide the comfort of structure, very sure definitions of success and failure, and the pleasure of having accomplishment inform one's identity. They are also the most closely aligned with the earthly rhythms of natural selection and survival of the fittest. Some cultures, in the extreme, provide for no redemption from failure and can truly be classified as shame cultures.

c) Grace and forgiveness, a self identity that believes **I am therefore I do.** This requires believing that you have a true and gifted identity that is not governed by circumstances, opinions, outcomes or even one's own failings, feelings and emotions – Jesus.

The Greek word for forgiveness means to set someone free, particularly from prison. Jesus didn't promise wealth, health, success, or freedom from problems, challenges or disaster. What he promised was release from the prison of failure and shame, and a new-born identity that will always be pure, beloved, honored and esteemed by Him and One's Creator. This message will likely endure forever because it has demonstrated its efficacy in freeing the human spirit to wear failure as a qualifying badge of honor rather than a disqualifying shame to bear. Once the human spirit with its heavenly identity is freed from the chains of earthly attempts to imprison it, all things are possible.

One caveat to this is that believers in Jesus will organize into a church with good intentions, and then sometimes perversely create their own shame culture and become like b) above. This is one of the greatest hinderances to the true message of Jesus.

Your friend,

Shan

Cover Photograph

The cover used for this book is a photograph of the author produced by Dave Gastineau in his final semester of college. David won many awards while obtaining a Bachelor of Fine Arts degree (Photography) from the Art Institute of Atlanta. Upon graduation, he was awarded Best in Show, which included this photograph among others.

Dave fell in love with cinema at a very young age, which in turn became a passion for imagery. While living in Oregon he got his first camera, allowing him to begin expressing his love for art. Dave lives in Atlanta, Georgia, is married to his wife Kara, has two children, Cameron and Quinlan, and works as a freelance photographer.

His website is davegastineau.com and his email is gastineaudave@gmail.com

About the Author

Shan Gastineau's earthly ID is as a Missouri-born Georgian who has no claim to fame. He graduated with honors from Georgia State University with a degree in Greek and Latin Classics while failing as a young pastor, husband and father. He has experienced both the dégradations of hell and exhilaration of heaven, and that is just referring to his two marriages to the same woman, though she may dispute the part about heaven.

Shan works in commercial real estate, specializing in corporate finance and portfolio advisory, but his real passion is challenging business leaders to look beyond success (or failure) to significance, especially eternal signicance.

Shan lives in Atlanta, Georgia with Lisa, his wife of 44 years, together sharing two sons and three grandchildren. Shan also has a daughter with special needs.

Notes

Foreword

1. P. Brickman and D.T. Campbell coined the term in their essay *Hedonic Relativism and Planning the Good Society (1971)*.

Introduction

2. Translated with comment by R.E. Allen, *The Symposium* (New Haven and London: Yale University Press, 1991), 54
3. Ibid., 55.
4. Dr. Nicole Rose, Mappalicious.com, *Feel Good vs. Feel Purpose*, 2016.
5. C.S. Lewis, The Weight of Glory essay, 1st paragraph.

Chapter I

6. Alfred North Whitehead, *Process and Reality*, p. 39, Free Press, 1979.

Chapter II

7. Matthew D. Lieberman, Naomi I. Eisenberger, Molly J. Crockett, Sabrina M. Tom, Jennifer H. Pfeifer, and Baldwin M. Way, *Putting Feelings into Words*, 2007, Psychological Science, Volume 18-Number 5, pgs. 421-428.
8. David Rock, *Your Brain at Work: Strategies for Overcoming Distraction, Regaining Focus, and Working Smarter All Day Long*, 2009
9. Ibid

Chapter IV

10. Translated by Hugh Tredennick, *Phaedo*, from *The Collected Dialogues of Plato* (Princeton NJ: Princeton University Press, 1989), 62.

11. Ibid, 64.

Chapter V

12. Translated with comment by R.E. Allen, *The Symposium* (New Haven and London: Yale University Press, 1991), 73

Chapter VI

13. Translated by Benjamin Jowett, *Symposium*, by Plato, (Midwest Journal Press), 74.

Chapter VII

14. Timothy Keller, *Galatians For You*, (The Good Book Company, 2013), 195-196.

15. H. Beck and C. Brown, DNTT, 2:776-83; J.I. Durham, *Proclamation and Presence: Old Testament Essays in Honor of Gwynne Henton Davies*; W. Eichrodt, *Theology of the Old Testament*; W. Foerster, TDNT, 2:400-420; D.J. Harris, *Shalom!: The Biblical Concept of Peace*; P.B. Yoder, Shalom: *The Bible's Word for Salvation, Justice, and Peace*.

Conclusion

16. Translated by Hugh Tredennick, *Phaedo*, from *The Collected Dialogues of Plato* (Princeton NJ: Princeton University Press, 1989), 68.

Made in the USA
Columbia, SC
13 November 2019